GW00854913

AWA Publishing

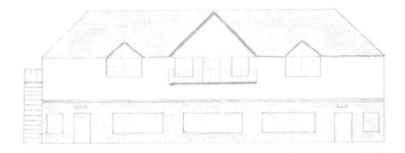

That's Bowls!

By L G Lanchris

For: all you bowlers out there.

CHAPTER ONE

The door to the Steward's flat above the Bowling Club creaked open and a small man with a balding head peered out, bleary brown eyes watering, blinking in the bright light of day. 'Ooh! Cor blimey,' uttered Dave Sirly, Club Steward as he stepped onto the open landing outside his flat, at the top of the wooden staircase. Dave scratched his unshaven chin below his scruffy grey moustache as he groped for the old wooden handrail on the stairs, trying to clear his head of last night's booze.

Dressed in an old tatty green shirt, with shiny blue trousers, the ends of which dragged along the floor at the back of his old scruffy brown slippers, Dave "Swirly" Sirly missed the next step and fell the last three, landing on his soft behind at the bottom of the staircase where he usually landed in the mornings. 'Ooh! Cor blimey,' uttered Dave as he dragged himself up and opened the wooden gate which led him onto the green of the bowls club.

Dave Sirly, or "Swirly" as he was usually known to the members of the Bowls Upper Morten Bowling Club liked a drink, a *good* drink, and sometimes when he'd had a good drink, when he was serving behind the club's bar, he turned quickly and 'swirled' right round, to face the wrong way. He'd been Steward of Bowls Upper Morten, or BUMs as it was known, for as long as he could remember, which was about two days, usually.

Dave walked by the frontage of the club, past the front of the bar and between himself and the electrified fence which surrounded the bowls green, which kept foxes, stray dogs, pigs and (many) drunken bowlers off the sacred grass, down to the door of the shop, with its golf clubs and bags, tees and dusty golfing paraphernalia. Originally Brigadier Stanley Accrington had bought a piece of land for a golf club; he had built the club and shop but ran out of money to purchase any more land, so compromised and used the ground for a six rink Bowls green.

Just before his death the Brigadier had left a will stating that as long as his descendants could operate the shop, with wages supplied by the clubs' committee, they could use his club for bowls. And the fat, lazy slug that was the Brigadier's great grandson, lazed in the shop most days, waiting for golf customers he knew would never come, but never stocked bowls equipment, as that would mean he would have to do some work.

Dave staggered by the shop, through the club room and into the large kitchen where his wife Amy, was preparing the dinner for the bowlers after today's game. Amy Sirly was a big woman, taller than Dave and twice, probably three times heavier than him with her dark hair drawn fiercely back behind her head, with large rosy cheeks, and she wore the white coat of the cook. This coat was undone down to four buttons at the front where her massive breasts billowed out like giant roller coaster waves of flesh. She poured another large glass of cooking sherry and swallowed the lot in one go. Her saucer like brown eyes widened and her big red mouth twisted into a great big grin when she turned and saw Dave. She strode towards him on her tree trunk like legs, swinging her great arms out and crushed his little body to her.

Dave found himself deep, deep in that enormous cleavage, ears bunged up with flesh, gasping for breath. 'Ooh! Cor blimey,' uttered Dave, stifled, as Amy "Zon" Sirly (for Amy-zon, or Amazon) crushed him to her.

Amy suddenly let Dave go by opening her arms quickly and pushing her great belly out. Dave was catapulted across the kitchen against the gas rings where the flames touched his already sore behind. 'An' don't forget, darlin', beamed Amy, 'big committee meeting tomorrow for the most important game of the season which happens shortly. The Grand Finale.'

'Ooh! Cor blimey,' uttered Dave.

Of the two hundred and eighty bowls clubs in the county of Cheswick, some were at the top of the tree of outstanding clubs, with restaurants, bars and cafes, some with many champions in singles, pairs, mixed pairs, triples, handicaps and so on. Other clubs had no amenities and few champions. One club was bowls club number two hundred and eighty, the last, the lowest ranked, the bottom rated club in the county. That club was Bowls Upper Morten: BUMs. On the last day of play each season, BUMs played the next lowest club in Cheswick county and always lost.

The Cheswick County league was built on the two up, two down policy, comprising the Elite Division, Division One, Division Two and so on until Division Thirteen, where BUM's had been for decades, in last place for the last twenty or so years. The local County newspaper "The Cheswick Daily Clarion" took great delight in the BUM's plight with headlines like "BUM's Hit Rock Bottom" and "Bum's On The Floor again", this year Pilkington Bowling Club had been demoted, causing them to have the same accrued points as BUM's. This game would be a play-off to see which was bottom; lose and you're last.

'Zat you, Dave?' a voice boomed from the bar area. Dave dusted himself down and shuffled forward from the kitchen into the club lounge, where the oak panels proudly showed in faded gold print the names of previous Presidents, Chairmen and Captains. And there he was; the President of the club, sitting at one of the tables munching nuts and crisps.

President Aldous "Aldolf" Hiller was large, very very large. He sat at the table on a wooden chair which was creaking and groaning under him, his thin grey hair seeming to grow all over his head, from whispy beard and moustache to very thin on top. His intimidating furrowed brow and glare from his reddish brown eyes, beaky nose and twisted mouth, were enough to frighten old ladies and children. His black shirt was stretched to its limit and could never really cover his enormous belly. When he stood, which was not very often, his giant behind looked like two moons covered in tightly stretched cloth.

'Yes, guv?' Dave shuffled in front of the table, 'you wanted to talk to me about something?'

'Yes Dave,' answered Aldous Hiller sternly, 'I do. At the committee meeting tomorrow, when we discuss the Finale, it is of the greatest importance; this time we *must* win. This time the next team above us in the listing, Pilkington Bowling Club, is playing here at home at BUMs. If we lose to them then we will be once again the lowest club in Cheswick. I'm not having it! We must win at all costs. Cheat them, beat them, poison them. We must win!'

'Good morning!' President and Steward twisted round at the sound of a voice from the club house's creaky doorway. A man had opened the door and entered the club. He was short and stocky, his greying hair was combed neatly back, and he sported a neatly clipped moustache and goatee beard. His bright blue eyes and his grinning mouth showed perfectly white and level teeth. He wore a white shirt and trousers with brown bowling shoes.

'You paid your two pound?' insisted President Hiller indignantly, with a sniff. 'All visitors got to pay two pound.'

'Well, actually,' beamed the new arrival, 'I'm Eddy. Eddy Edmunds. I've finished my training at another club, but I've since moved into this area. So I'm not a visitor, I'm a new member.'

'A new Member!' BUMs President and Steward exploded together in pure astonishment.

'Yes, I am,' smiled Eddy, 'and I thought I'd drop in to pay my Membership fee, if it's alright to do so today.'

'Ahh,' smiled Aldous Hiller, with a crafty wink at Dave, 'if you aint paid yer Membership yet, you still got to pay your two quid visitor fee. So that's two quid.' He held out his hand,

and stared threateningly.

'But I'm here to pay my membership fee,' sputtered Eddy.

'So that's two quid as a visitor and a hundred quid Membership. Hundred and two quid,' insisted Aldous, pushing his open hand under Eddy's chin. 'Then, once you've joined we can talk about what competitions you wanna go in for, and charge you for each individual one. One hundred and two quid. You can always claim back your visitor's two quid, at, er, next years AGM. Cash or card?'

'Er, I thought I'd go to the hole in the wall machine once I find out who I pay, and pay cash.'

'Paying in cash?' Aldous grinned. 'That'll be me, then.'

'Will I get a locker?' Eddy asked, 'I'd like somewhere to put my gear, if I can, so a locker would be handy.'

'Me, me, me some people,' Aldous spat out disgustedly, 'all right, I'll get you a locker, forty quid a season. That's a hundred and forty two quid, then, and if its in cash then, you can pay, er, me.'

'Oh, oh, I see,' Eddy looked worried, 'a hundred and forty two quid, still, it'll be worth being able to lock away my woods and stuff.'

'Lock away!' Aldous was disgusted, 'you want a *lockable* locker. You want a key? OK, OK, with a key then. That'll be another ten quid per season, then. A hundred and fifty two quid. Cash you said. Now.'

'Erm, OK, OK,' Eddy turned, 'I'll just go to the cash machine in the town. I'll be back soon.'

'Just get the money, son.' Aldous leaned back in the creaking chair.

CHAPTER TWO

'That's sixteen pounds sixty seven pence then, please,' gasped Dave as he delivered the second heavy tray of drinks to the table where the committee were sitting.

'Wotja, mean?' rasped Aldous Hiller angrily, as he eased his bulk into the creaking chair, 'you can't ask a duly authorised committee member to *pay* for his or her first drinks!'

'Well ... well, I mean,' Dave squirmed unhappily, 'it's not exactly your *first* round is it, guv?'

'Yes it is!' exploded Aldous, his little reddish eyes almost popping out of his big, grey head.

'No. No, guv,' simpered Dave, beginning to sweat, 'this is the second round I've brought you to this table today.'

'Yes, yes,' Aldous thundered, 'I know it's the second round you've brought to this committee table, but it's the first round for *me*. It's *my* first drink, and club rules clearly state that when on club business, you get your first drink free. And this is *my* first drink, and I'm just including in a few friends, who are after all, on the same committee.'

'Yes, guv,' spluttered Dave, almost in tears, 'but it's the second time I've got this round for you-'

'No. No. You don't understand,' Aldous talked quietly as though teaching a slightly dopey child, 'this is *my* first round, *my* first free drink. The last time you brought the drinks to this table, I didn't order that round. My good friend and colleague did, the erstwhile Captain Horatio Anchor. So go away Dave, but come back soon, 'cos the other two people sitting at this committee table have yet to order their first drinks, which will be free, as club rules and regulations clearly state.' Dave shuffled off, leaving the committee to continue its meeting.

This meeting, The Allotments and Gardens Committee, was always held before any visiting bowls team came to Bowls Upper Morten for a match. It was a committee of war and attrition.

Around the table with the bloated Aldous Hiller were his good friend Captain Horatio Anchor, also known as Captain Horatio- well, you can guess the rest. Captain Anchor was a tall, bald man with his last remaining whisps of head hair shaved off, a wet mouth and sad brown eyes; he wore an old check shirt and dirty white trousers, with old brown boots. He had spent many years in the Royal Navy, serving in submarines, and worked his way up the promotions ladder until he became Captain of the submarine *Intrepid*. All went well until on his first mock battle, he ordered "Dive. Dive. Dive." but forgot to shut the door.

After leaving the Navy under a cloud, (sixty feet of water actually), he took a post at Peckham's Public School for boys as Bursar. At the school he was surprised to find that most of the boys gave him all the money that their parents had given them for the term, to look after. And the school Headmaster gave him cash to invest for the coming term, like food, extra books and outings for the boys, and other masters also entrusted him with their cash. At the end of his first week as Bursar, the large table in his office was awash with stashed cash; neatly stacked fifty pound notes, twenty pound notes, boxes with cash stuffed inside, and even carrier bags of money littered the table top. And that's exactly what he told the police the next day, when he came in and all the cash was gone. Leaving the Bursars job at the school was similar to Horatio Anchor leaving the navy: forgetting to shut the door.

Next around the committee table was club Treasurer, Price Watergate, "Pricey". Always called "Mister" when spoken to, was Mister Price Watergate, as he was a true gentleman; always courteous and polite, always immaculately dressed in a suit with a waistcoat, brilliant white shirt, colour-coded tie and sparkling shoes. A relatively small man, but one who stood out in a crowd, his slicked back silvery hair, trimmed every fortnight, his honest brown eyes looking intently around, his clean shaven chin and face seemingly scrubbed clean and shiny. His opinion on any subject was totally honest and direct. Today he sat relaxed, sipping his gin and tonic, his light blue tie complementing his dark blue suit and waistcoat. He would be all in perfect white when he was on the green, playing bowls.

The final person at the table for the committee meeting was Men's Bowls Captain Fergus O'Brien, "Mad Mick". The ex-Irish Rugby International player, who told everyone about his International games as often as possible, was indeed a very good bowler, but sadly, had never lost his broad Irish accent. When he spoke, he was extremely difficult to understand, especially when he was at the head, instructing his team on where to aim, with animated howls and gestures. This accounted for the nickname "Mad Mick". Fergus sat at the table with pints of porter in front of him, with his thick, wavy greying hair and his bright patchy-skinned red face, thick bushy eyebrows, long sideburns and big, open mouth. He gripped his pint in his thick fingers and swallowed deep, his old checked shirt sagging out of his brown belt, over brown corduroy trousers, on his feet were large scuffed boots.

'Now then,' slurped Aldous Hiller, releasing a large burp as he spoke, 'we got a home game against Wellerton Bowling Club tomorrow, and next week will be the final against Pilkington for the bottom of the ratings. We must use the Wellerton game as a practice session for the big one, the final against Pilkington.

'Tasselated boob jobs!' Mad Mick roared, with a flat handed smack on the table top, 'Dinosaur poo and rabids!' Mick looked accusingly around the table. The other three at the meeting gave sagely nodded agreement to whatever it was he had just uttered.

'I gotta plan!' Aldous looked round the club room to see if anyone was in earshot, then beckoned the three to lean closer. They did. He whispered: 'All park your cars awkwardly in the car park and in the road outside. Make the frail old buggers from Wellerton park their cars a long way off and then carry their bowls up the gravel path, that'll wear them out before they play. And on the green, drop your woods on their toes.' All at the table tittered and giggled.

'Of course,' said Pricey Watergate, 'we couldn't really do that, could we? I mean, that'd be cheating wouldn't it?'

'Oh, of course not,' Aldous sneakily smiled, 'we wouldn't really do it, would we lads?' He winked to everyone else at the table with a knowing nod. 'And I notice that Peter Travers has come up with a clever idea to modernise Bowls Upper Morten's web page, with automatic updates and results.'

'What does he know?' spat Horatio in disgust, 'he's only been a member for seven or eight years, and he's not on any one of the club's committees. What are we going to do about him?'

'He'll have to go, of course,' answered Aldous, 'we were going to do that on the web-page ourselves anyway. But what I say is: If it ain't broke, don't mend it.'

'Actually, of course, I'm being picky, I know,' said Pricey rubbing a hand through his silver hair, 'but the web-page *is* broke, isn't it?'

'No it ain't broke!' Aldous blurted angrily.

'Yes it is broke!' they all chorused back.

'Brassier's grope!' agreed Mad Mick.

'Well,' smoothed in Pricey, 'when you look in onto our bowls club web-page, all that lightens up the page is an advert for a minicab company, which was a good idea of yours Aldous, to get sponsorship from a minicab company. So, in one way at least, the one way being that you can't locate the bowls club, then it *is* broke. It does make sense for the club web-page to tell us something about the club, to give members information about upcoming games and results.'

'Yes, I know all that,' winked Aldous, 'but what information our dear members haven't got, they can't alter. We control it all. Believe me, it ain't broke.'

'Hi, chaps!' called a cheery voice from the doorway, 'just having a look around my new club.'

'Oooze that?' cried Pricey and Horatio.

'Popcorn 'ee?' asked Fergus.

'That's Eddy Edmunds, he's a new member!' Aldous Hiller boomed proudly. 'An' he's all paid up in full.'

'You mean,' said Pricey, incredulously, 'he's paid the full amount, up front and at this late date in the season?'

'Yes, he certainly has,' smarmed Adolf Hiller, 'and here's the full twenty quid as a pro rata payment,' he said laying two ten pound notes out in front of Pricey, the Treasurer.

'Ahem!' coughed Dave Swirly as he swept by with an accusing look at BUMs President Hiller, who responded with a glare of death at Dave. Eddy Edmunds blissfully wandered by.

CHAPTER THREE

Eddy Edmunds wandered happily through the crumbling club, noting the whereabouts of the toilets, the bar opening times, and the many notices and 'coming events' on the notice board. Some of the jumbled pieces of paper pinned, taped or blue tacted to the board seemed very old and tatty. He read one, a dinner-dance in December which stated that it was for the Kings Coronation, and another for a cinema evening to see a new movie, 'Gone With The Wind'.

'Hulloooo!' sang a voice from behind Eddy, 'how can I help you?' Eddie swung round to see a lady, who had been dashing by, skid to a stop. She had short and curly brown hair, popping eyes and a wide smile with very long teeth all in a face that had never seen make up. She wore a pearl necklace, a Tweed jacket and skirt, thick stockings covered her thick legs and on her feet were flat brown shoes. This lady was all jolly hockey sticks.

'Hello, I'm Eddy Edmunds,' Eddy began with a large grin, 'I'm a new bowling member at BUMs.'

'Ha ha! New member eh,' laughed the woman, with a gurgling snort, 'new member, but, here? Now? Why? I, I, I mean, how lovely. Welcome to Bowls Upper Morten. I'm Gladys Glendenning, and everybody calls me GG. I'm Captain of the ladies team. Anything you want, all you have to do is ask. I do, you know. I do, everything and anything … for anybody.'

'Everything … anything … for anybody?' Eddy said with a fearful frown, looking for an exit.

'Yes, I do,' said GG, 'I mow the green, tend to the flowers, clean the club and the toilets, shine the windows, organise the fund raising, call the bingo, sell the raffle tickets, empty the bins, serve behind the bar when needed, open the club in the morning and close it at night. Oh, and I captain the ladies' team of course.' GG then raced off on her next job of work for the Bowls Club.

Eddy peered into old glass cases where the club silverware was on display. The few cups that were on show were faded and the engraving on them could hardly be seen behind misty glass, and the photographs of previous club games and festivals looked ancient in black and white.

Eddy wandered outside. Alongside the club, on the raised flooring by the green, leaning against the wall were large cupboards. As they were unlocked, Eddy idly opened the doors as he walked by and peered in. In open boxes in the cupboards were white and yellow solid balls, which were the 'Jacks' which were aimed at in the game of bowls, while in another open box were right angled pieces of steel, some painted white and some painted red. These were 'Irons' used for hanging over the side of the ditch, pointing at a Jack or a wood which had landed there.

'Stand still that man!' roared a voice from behind. 'You there! The man by the jacks and irons! Stop! Stop I say!' Eddy froze. Then, gathering his composure, slowly turned to see who had shouted at him.

The man who had shouted was small. Curly white hair covered his head, while accusing, staring dark eyes glared out over a large nose and pursed lips. He wore a white shirt with blue tie, dark blue sports blazer, grey trousers and buckled shoes. 'That's the jacks and irons!' he roared as he marched in a threatening military fashion towards Eddy, 'I'm in charge of jacks and irons!' He shook with rage as he spoke, seemingly ready to blow a fuse, or his heart to fly out of his chest. 'Don't touch the jacks and irons! He bellowed, his face turning puce.

'It's alright, my friend,' soothed Eddy, 'I'm a new member. Just wandering round my new club, taking a look. I wasn't going to touch-'

'I'm in charge of jacks and irons!' the little man roared on, 'no one touches ... you're a new member? A *new* member?

What here at Bowls Upper Morten? But why? I, er, I mean, great! Welcome. Jackson Irons.'

'Yes, I know,' groaned Eddy, 'you already said, you're in charge of jacks and irons. You did mention that, I think.'

'Yes, yes,' smiled the small man, calming down, 'Jackson Irons, that's me, I'm in charge of jacks and irons and it's me name: Jackson Irons. See, jacks and irons keep going missing, so Adolf ... I mean Aldous Hiller, our illustrious President gave me the job of handing them out and keeping a running total, to make sure we've got 'em all. It just happens to be my name as well. Jackson Irons.'

'I see, thanks for explaining,' said Eddy, his mind in a spin, 'well I'm Eddy Edmunds-' At that moment Eddy's eyes strayed a bit further along the club wall and saw a number of pushers, the white painted wheeled scoops, which were hanging on hooks. 'And tell me,' Eddy strolled over to the pushers and gently tugged at one, 'you haven't got a player here called Pusher, have you?'

'No one touches the pushers!' screamed Jackson Irons, 'I hand those out, no one else! I'm in charge of the pushers!' Eddy backed away from the little man, and scurried along. Later, at the bar, he bought a drink and asked the Steward, Dave Sirly about Jackson Irons.

'Oh, Jackson Irons,' smiled Dave, 'I'd forgotten that was his name, I only know him by his nickname.'

'What's his nickname?' asked Eddy as he downed his pint.

'Pusher.'

CHAPTER FOUR

Eddy Edmunds was excited. This could be his first match coming up. At last, he could put his name down on the list of players for the Bowls Upper Morten game against Wellerton. All you had to do was go to the notice board where the up coming games were listed and put your name down early enough, and Presto! if they picked your name out, you played.

Eddy scoured the notice board. There it was! A card with the date and time of the match, and where it was to be played; just put your name down. This was a home game for six rinks, next Sunday. Eddy penned his name in happily.

Each time he entered the club after he had put his name down for the Wellerton game, Eddy checked the list, and each day more and more names of his team-mates had been added to the list.

Then one day, the list for the Wellerton game disappeared. The Captains and the Match Secretary must be selecting the teams! It was all very exciting! Eddy turned and saw the Match Secretary walking towards him, waving a small rectangle of card in his hand. It had to be the list of teams! He was going to pin it up on the wall! Eddy felt a rush of excitement as the man approached.

Match Secretary Jason Cable was big man, middle-aged and was completely bald on top of his head, so he had allowed the ring of thick, stringy dark hair which still grew in a ring from above his ears to the back of his neck to continue to grow to straggly shoulder-length proportions. His dull pasty blue eyes squinted dully above a short pug nose, his round chin covered in three days growth of dark beard. His blue club blazer, festooned with badges, brooches and clips of many metals and colours was tatty and grubby. The shirt he wore beneath his blazer had tattered cuffs and inside the open collar was a ring of grime. His old black trousers were shiny and stopped two inches from his ankles, showing beneath a pair of scruffy, once white trainers.

Jason "Scruffbag" Cable marched importantly along to the notice board and pinned up the list of players. 'Ooh!' cried Eddy, 'I'm on the list! I'm playing!'

'You the new bloke?' asked Jason, in an uninterested sort of way, hammering the drawing pins into the wall with a crash.

'Yes …' Eddy became aware of the powerful smell of body odour which seemed to fill the area where they stood, making him heave.

'Right. It's all organised,' said Scruffbag with supreme confidence, 'you're number three to Winnie Wilson's four.'

'But that list says I'm playing at number two,' Eddy pointed to the list, trying not to hold his nose.

'Eh? Oh yeah,' laughed the Match Secretary, taking out a biro from his top pocket and scrubbing out Eddy's name. Then he scrubbed out the number one's name and inserted Eddy's name there. 'Right, that's you sorted, but now I gotta change the number one I had in Winnie's team to just … there!' He scrubbed out another name on a different team and inserted the new name. 'Ahh,' he mused, 'I'll put him in here,' he scrubbed more names out, 'an' her in there …' and inserted new names as he crossed through names and scribbled in new ones. Very soon the now dog-eared list of players was full of unintelligible crossings out.

'We OK now?' asked Eddy, staring at the limp list of players.

'Sorted.' Match Secretary Jason "Scruffbag" Cable announced and then marched away, onto his next bit of club organising. Eddy stared long and hard at the mutilated list, but could make no sense of it at all.

A man came into the club and stood beside him and also stared at the list. 'Hullo!' Eddy chirped, 'I'm Eddy Edmunds. I'm a new club member.' Eddy extended his right hand in greeting.

'And *I'm* Kirkland Dunne,' said the man, not accepting Eddy's proffered handshake, 'And I'm the number one player of this bowls club. You *must* have heard of me if you've been in this club for more than two minutes.'

'Erm ... yes, of course,' Eddy lied as he took a good look at the man. Kirkland Dunne, known as "Number One" was not tall, but stood proud, smiling like a movie star being interviewed, with scruffy, wavy hair, deep set brown eyes, surrounded by soft, saggy skin. He wore a bright red T-shirt upon the back of which, in giant white letters announced: NUMBER ONE BOWLER. He wore old, scruffy green track suit bottoms and battered white trainers.

'See that wall down there?' Kirkland ordered, pointing to the far wall of the club house, where all the previous winners' names were painted on the wooden panelling. 'See that wall? My name's on that wall more than any other player at BUMs. Singles, pairs, mixed pairs, triples, handicaps and fours, I've won 'em all. Me. An' one year, I'll win all the lot in the same season. Then they'll acknowledge what I already know. Kirkland Dunne is the best bowler there is. I'll be as famous a bowler as Francis Drake.

'An' look what that stupid Scruffbag has done.' Kirkland drew out a large red marker pen and crossed through a name on the list of players for the Wellerton game and wrote in the position of number four, or Skip: Kirkland Dunne.

CHAPTER FIVE

Saturday afternoon, and Eddy walked into the club for a drink and a chat before the big day of his first tournament the following day. He glanced at the list of the team members on the wall as he entered, which was still full of the scribblings of Jason "Scruffbag" Cable, and what looked like more entries and crossings out. Still, he could see his name on Winnie Wilson's team as number one. He strode on into the club.

After buying himself a pint from Dave Sirly, Eddy wandered into the club where two elderly ladies, dressed in their white skirts and blue BUMs blazers adorned with many badges and brooches, pin-on Union Jacks and bowling pins, were pulling tables with folded legs into the dance floor area and unfolding them with much puffing and blowing, and were then pulling and pushing them into position for tomorrow's dinner after the game with Wellerton.

Eddy, carrying his pint, turned to sit in the glass roofed area where people would sit inside the club and watch a match, when the weather was chilly or raining and they didn't want to sit outside. Nearby, two ladies were having a heated conversation. Eddy sat down in one of the comfortable armchairs which lined the conservatory part of the club, not looking at the ladies, but could not avoid being able to hear what was being said between the two.

One lady was Gladys Glendenning who Eddy had met already, the other was Lily Puddle, a plump, older lady, known as "Lily Lips" because apparently she never stopped talking. Gladys was in her usual Tweed while Lily's grey hair was swept under a scarf, her staring grey eyes looked out over a bulging nose and twittering mouth. Her body was wrapped in a large white cardigan and white skirt which reached her ankles, and on her feet were blue bumpers.

'Well, you know,' babbled Lily, 'it's not like it was and

I've got the TV man coming round later on 'cos I can't get channel five sometimes unless I crank the aerial round against the bird cage but it upsets Polly and I haven't had a working phone since Wednesday or was it Tuesday and the corner shops shut it wasn't like that in my day I can tell you and the lens fell out of me glasses so I thought I'd come and help you out today 'cos it's doctor's Monday.'

'Yes, yes,' GG was fraught, 'but you've mowed the green. I always mow the green, especially before a match. You should never-'

'Well I said I'd help,' Lily went on, 'they wouldn't have stood for it in my day especially with the rationing I was going to get a lift from old Tom but he can't drive he's heads swollen up to three times its size and he can't get in the car or was it his leg an' I have to get three buses to get here and one o' thems a Hale and Pace or is it a Hail and Ride so I mowed the green for you.'

'Yes Lily,' sighed a tearful GG, 'but you mowed it in circles! Round and round! Haven't you ever noticed that we mow diagonally?

Outside on the green Captain Mad Mick stared in disbelief at the grass as he scratched his grey head and mumbled: 'Cod in batter!'

'So now I've lost me lens,' continued Lily without a stop, 'I've got me Readers and me Lookers, but no Shoppers or Seer's an' I got the doctor's on Monday not that he understands English an' I got a leaking tap but the man can't come round till Thursday so I sellotaped it up Ooo there's Ginny Oooh Ginny.' Without a stop in her talking Lily moved off to see Ginny.

'Oh well,' sighed GG with a tear, 'perhaps I'll come in early tomorrow before the game and mow the grass again and hope that no one notices it.'

At the other end of the club, the two elderly ladies, the

Blagett sisters, had now finished unfolding the long tables and pulling them into position for the tomorrow's after-game dinner, and were now exhaustedly puffing and blowing, and sitting on the tables after all the physical effort of positioning them and were resting before putting out all the chairs around the tables. They were approached by Winnie Wilson, the lady who would be Eddy's Skip at tomorrow's game.

Winnie "Witch" Wilson was ancient, she had been a member of BUMs since anyone could remember, she was not tall and appeared frail, and her whispy white hair stuck out like a straw on a scarecrow, her skin was wrinkly and yellow, contrasted by her red mouth which was caked with lipstick, but her eyes and her manner were steely. She wore, as always, her smart blue BUMs blazer and white trousers and trainers. 'Well, girls,' she looked hard at the two helper ladies, 'nice job unfolding all the tables for the after-game dinner for tomorrow, but you're too previous. There's bingo tonight and all these tables will be in the way. They'll have to go back.' She marched away.

'Witch!' whispered one of the elderly ladies.

'Old moaner!' sighed the other, as they dragged themselves up and began folding the tables back up and stacking them in the corner.

The club door crashed open and the large Amy Sirly marched in, dragging with her carrier bags full of big tins of peas, beans, pounds and pounds of potatoes, bottles and bottles of cooking oil and sherry, and many other items she needed to prepare the meal for tomorrow. She crashed past the ladies folding up the tables and marched into the kitchen, where she deposited her bags onto the work tops, crashed back outside again, only to re-appear, minutes later, with more bags to put into the kitchen. All the while her white 'cook's coat trailed behind her, the usual four buttons undone showing massive cleavage, bobbing up and down rhythmically.

'Well,' thought Eddy, 'the club's certainly coming to life in readiness for the game tomorrow. He finished his pint and prepared to leave. He stood up, and taking his empty glass back to the bar, turned to the door and bumped into Winnie Wilson, who was marching back in.

'Ahh,' Winnie gave Eddy a cold stare, 'you're the new boy at the club, aren't you, Eddy Edwards.'

'Edmunds, actually,' smiled Eddy, 'pleased to-'

'Better make a good showing, tomorrow Edwins,' Winnie commanded, poking Eddy in the chest with a bony finger, 'Oh ladies!' she cried, peering round the side of Eddy, down to the other end of the club, 'you don't have to put all the tables back! It's bingo tonight! We'll need a couple of tables out for the number machine! Unfold some again! My God! Do I have to do everything myself!' Winnie marched off.

CHAPTER SIX

Sunday morning arrived, the day of the game against the visiting team of Wellerton BC. At the dance floor end of the club, the two elderly ladies, Dotty and Betty Blagett, as usual dressed in their white skirts and blue BUMs blazers were once again pulling the folded tables onto the dance floor and unfolding them with much puffing and blowing, and then pulling and pushing them into position for today's dinner after the friendly game with Wellerton.

Nicholas Chambers marched into the club, his little legs carrying him quickly towards the kitchen, his screwed up little face stared before him in anger, the few remaining hairs on his head flowing along behind. He wore a full length white macintosh which covered him from neck to knees, over his large belly, while below, his little legs pumped him along like a duck in water. His furrowed brows above dark little eyes made a V in his narrow forehead, with his pointy nose like a sharpened arrow. His down-turned little mouth looked at the world in disgust, in disgust that everything about him was higher than he was. It seemed that everyone in the world was taller than him. Everyone looked down on him and they all had to pay. 'Outa my way!' he roared at the two elderly ladies working on the tables.

'Oh, pooh! On yer bike!' cried one old girl, old Dotty Blagett.

'Look out everyone!' shouted the other old lady, old Betty, 'Old Nick's coming through.' Both the ladies laughed and carried on, as both knew that Old Nick Nasty Chambers was as deaf as a post. Pauline Chambers, Old Nick's long suffering wife had made a career of apologising and making excuses for her husbands bad temper and manners, earning for herself the nickname of Chambers Pot.

'I wonder why he's so nasty.' asked table lady Dotty, as

they continued to pull out the folded tables and stand them up.

'Yers,' answered Betty, twisting up the metal legs of a table, 'I mean, he's retired now, but he used to travel in ladies' underwear.'

'Really!' laughed Dotty, locking back the legs of a table, 'praps that's what gave the nasty little sausage the hump!'

'No,' giggled Betty, 'he travelled, you know, a travelling salesman, in ladies' underwear. He didn't wear it, well, I don't think so!' The two collapsed into guffaws of laughter.

Old Nick burst into the kitchen where he glared at Amy "Zon" Sirly, 'Here!' he shouted, 'if you're going to cook for a crowd of people, you've got to have certificates! Health and Safety Certificates!'

'Shut your face,' Amy answered with a smile as she turned towards him, 'you deaf old sod!'

'Whassat?' he said, 'what'd you say?' Amy grabbed the little man to her and hugged him into her cleavage.

'I said,' she shouted onto the back of his head, 'Pucker up. We'll have a snog.' She crushed him to her breasts until his breathing became laboured. Then she let him go and pumped out her belly at the same time. He staggered back, red faced, fighting for breath. Amy led him to the kitchen doorway, opened the door and pushed and bundled him unceremoniously through the gap, closed the door on him with a bang and went back to her cooking preparations.

BUMs players began to arrive at the club house, the men wearing club blazers and white trousers, the ladies in their blazers and white skirts or trousers. Some of the older members seemed quite frail and elderly, while others looked confused and lost. Some carried heavy rucksacks with their whites, in which everyone had to play or hauled behind them a shopping trolley, filled with their needs, and medicines and tablets to keep them going.

Dave served busily behind the bar, as club members

arrived and ordered their one and only drink and greeted other members with rigorous hand shaking for the men and wet, sloppy kisses for the ladies, as if they hadn't seen each other for ages, when of course, they had seen each other at the bingo yesterday.

Players crowded around the lists of forthcoming games, jostling for position, adding their names to the number of players "on the list" of available people for the games. Horatio Anchor wandered the growing crowd, smiling and nodding at the faces he knew, and waving like royalty to everyone.

Gladys Glendenning marched round the club and ladies changing rooms, geeing up the ladies, handing out useless information and grinning a toothy grin, and then marching around leading the ladies onwards.

Outside, Jackson Irons laid out the pushers, jacks, irons, mats and score boards on the grass in rows, while fiercely flashing deadly looks at anyone who might touch one of his closely guarded implements.

Fergus O'Brien waved on the mainly elderly gentlemen players of the BUMs team, helping them along with cheery remarks for a good game, like: 'Tootle main. It'll be a bike!'

At the bar, the unwary got caught as Lily "Lips" Puddle recounted her day so far: 'Well o course I could 'ave gone to the Wellerton but I like it here and my operation at the hospital didn't go well I mean it aint as if it's Friday an my telly works now I found the remote in me husbands ashes under the cat...'

Among the many bald and grey heads milling about in the club house, as the playing members arrived for the game in their badge-covered blazers and baseball caps, Jason Cable swung his lank hair this way and that as he instructed members as to where on the green they would be playing and with whom, pointing first to one rink, then the next, leaving people even more confused than they had been before they asked his guidance as Match Secretary.

'What d'yer think then, Pricey?' Aldous Hiller asked from his creaking chair, 'looks like a good turn out, so far.'

'Yes, and the Wellerton team hasn't arrived yet,' Pricey Watergate answered, looking cool in his white bowling suit and shining white shoes, his silver hair slicked down in perfect style.

'Well, I couldn't help it,' smirked Aldous, sipping his long drink and popping just a few more cheese biscuits into his sloppy mouth, 'if my car blocked the car park, and the poor old visitors from Wellerton will have to park down the road a bit, after the yellow lines,' At that point a sweating head peered into the club room. A tiny ancient Wellerton player, a frail man well into his eighties staggered in, dragging behind him a very heavy looking trolley, full of white bowling outfit and four woods.

'Gawd!' the old boy gasped as he staggered in, 'it's a long way from where the double yellow lines end to this club house.' Adolf Aldous Hiller stuck out his foot.

CHAPTER SEVEN

Now the day was really warming up, the Wellerton players puffed, sweated and trudged into the BUMs club room, got themselves a cool drink at the bar and made their way to the changing rooms.

On the dance floor area, the table ladies had at last finished putting up the tables and shoving in the chairs for the after game dinner, and sat themselves down for a celebratory gin and tonic. 'What on earth are you girls doing?' demanded a by now red faced Horatio Anchor as he ambled by, waving to the newly crowded club house, 'you know you've got to leave the top two rows of tables round the other way for the raffle after the game.' He tutted as he walked on, greeting the arriving players.

'Oh, pooh,' sighed old Betty and Dotty together, as they pulled themselves up and began to manoeuvre tables once more.

By now, Aldous Hiller was lumbering his round frame along with the players working their way to the changing rooms. 'Now be careful, lads and lasses,' he called, 'don't touch the fence around the green, it's electrified and is still switched on. Me and Old Nick'll turn it off then you can fall over it all you want, but at least it won't fry you. And if you actually give us time, we'll remove the fence, then you can fall straight onto the green if you want.' Aldous waddled on, followed by Old Nick, tiny legs pumping below the inevitable white coat.

The electrified fence was made of four one inch wide strands of white material which were strung between posts at each corner of the green and held in place by other removable posts along the rinks and when switched on carried an extremely nasty electric shock from its bottom strand two inches from the ground to the top of the four strands four feet high.

At last the two pushed themselves through the crowd of

pensioners, who were shuffling into the ladies or men's changing rooms, making the usual comments about going into the wrong changing room and de-robing for all to see.

In a small alleyway between the two changing rooms, Aldous roughly pushed Old Nick down to where a large rubber-covered metal handle protruded. The handle could be left in one of two positions; at the top where there was printed a large label which read: OFF, and the other position, at the bottom, which read ON. Aldous pushed Old Nick further down the alleyway until he was under the handle, which was pointing down to the ON position.

'Now,' shouted Aldous, 'when I say "Now", turn the handle.'

'Eh? What?' Old Nick bad temperedly answered, a hand cupping his ear, 'what'd you just say?'

'Oh, Gawd 'elp us.' Aldous gasped, 'You daft, deaf old sod! Listen to me! When I say "Now"-'

'Now?' asked Old Nick, 'when you say "Now"?'

'Yes, when I say "Now"!' Crash! Old Nick slammed up the handle.

'No, you old fool,' cried Aldous, 'not now, not now, do it when I say "Now", oh, what does it matter, you've done it now.'

'It's no good you saying now, now,' Old Nick muttered despairingly, 'you've already said now, now, and I've done it now.'

With an exasperated look up into the sky, Aldous turned and waved for Jackson Irons and Jason Cable to go around the green, collecting up the four tapes of the electric fence and their holders, to be stored away until after the game, when it would be put back to keep the precious green safe from the countryside foxes, cattle, badgers, pigs and drunken players.

Jackson Irons began to fold up the electrical fence tapes, pulling out the supporting posts as he went, while Jason Cable did the same at the other end of the green. Jackson was the first to trip on the trailing tapes and crashed to the green on top of the irons, jacks and mats that he should have laid out *after* the electrical fence was put away. Jason thought it was hilarious that Jackson tripped over the trailling tapes until he also tripped on the masses of tapes he had gathered up in his arms. Eventually they jammed the bundled and twisted electrical tapes in the alleyway between the changing rooms and left it for someone else to sort out after the game.

Inside the men's changing room, old Charlie Higginbottom struggled to pull off his blazer and shirt, pulling first at his sleeves and then peeling the clothes off his sweating back. Charlie was no longer a young man, or even a middle aged man, tall, thin and bony with great tufts of dirty grey hair which sprang from his ears and down from his nose in long grey twists, but not from his bald head. His tall, thin frame was also filled with lumps, man boobs, pot belly, sticky-out bum and his arms and legs had layers of empty, flappy skin. All of this was usually hidden beneath loose-fitting clothes.

Charlie dropped his shirt and blazer onto a bench already full of other peoples clothes, and unbuckled his belt and dropped his trousers. 'Ooh,' cried Charlie as a cool wind brushed him, 'I've dropped me pants as well as me trousers. I'll have to bend over and pick me pants up.' Charlie stood naked in the crowded changing room, his grey sagging flesh and lumpy belly and bum for all to see.

'No! No Charlie! Don't do it!' shouted the men in the changing room, 'don't bend down!' Too late. Charlie bent stiff-legged down for his dirty grey pants, sticking his bum up in the air.

'Eeuurrgh!' cried the men who couldn't help looking.

'I can see where all your hair went from your head Charlie!' cried an old wag.

Jackson Irons finally caught up with the Blagett sisters as they made their way from the ladies changing room. 'Ladies!

Ladies!' Jackson cried as he saw them, 'Emergency instructions from our leader, Mr Aldous Hiller.'

'What now?' the Blagett sisters said together.

'The Hon Sec says someone left the electrical fence in a mess, stuffed between the changing rooms, and he needs his best, most helpful and loyal helpers to sort it out so it can be put back up at the end of the game. That's you.' Jackson smiled a creepy smile and disappeared.

'Oh, pooh,' Dotty Blagett sighed.

'It's always us,' Betty agreed.

CHAPTER EIGHT

Eddy Edmunds was really getting excited now, as all of the players, both BUMs and Wellerton were gathering on the outside of the club house against the green dressed in their white tops and white trousers, or for the ladies, sometimes skirts. Jackson Irons had once again laid out the irons, mats and jacks as the men and women took their wines and beers outside to stand chattering, smoking and drinking, waiting for the two opposing Captains to make an appearance, while a small cloud of bluish cigarette smoke hovered above their heads.

Back in the club house, at the dance floor end, Dotty and Betty Blagett pushed the last chair under the last table and turned to the door into the changing rooms.

'What are you two doing?' demanded Gladys "GG" Glendenning as she raced by, big legs stamping her feet on the floor, 'all those tables are round the wrong way, they should be longitude not latitude. Really!' The sisters sat down at a table in disbelief.

At last, the Captains appeared on the green. Fergus O'Brien strode out with the Wellerton Captain, Jerome "Jerry" Cann, both Captains carried score books with them listing who was playing from their team on which rink. Jerry was a tall man in his early seventies and incredibly untidy. His thin head which seemed to narrow as it went up was sparsely covered in flying, stringy dark hair, his narrow eyes darted fervently everywhere accusingly, as fluffy black eyebrows fluttered above. His long bony nose was crookedly poised above a downturned, twisted mouth on his unshaven chin. A creased and dirty white-ish shirt was tucked into baggy greyish white trousers on his large belly, and one sleeve of the shirt was rolled up to the elbow, the other sleeve had rolled down. His dirty, greasy, black shoes were originally white.

'Afternoon, everyone,' Jerry said in a loud voice, 'and

thanks to Upper Morten for inviting us here today. It's a crucial game, I know, so's you can sort out who you'll field in your big match with Pilkington next week, cos I know you'll not want to be the two hundred and eightieth club of two hundred and eighty in Cheswick county … again.' Jerry raised a hand to his mouth in a theatrical attempt to hide a smirk. All the Wellerton players roared with laughter. 'On rink one,' Jerry continued, reading carefully from his score-book, 'is Marlene Moss, Joanny Stiller …' He read out the four names of the team.

'Heinous blinking,' read Mad Mick Fergus from his score-books, 'Eddy Midus…' he continued to read the first score-book, which no-one understood, and when Fergus handed the score-book to Winnie Wilson they gathered round to find out who was playing under her as Skip.

When all the score-books were handed out to the two teams there followed a great confusion, as people learned what rink they were playing on and in what position and began to move bowls and drinks, waterproof coats, jumpers and cardigans back and forth across the green, bumping into each other, knocking chairs, cigarettes and drinks onto the ground as they did so. The two Captains wandered back to the bar while the players took twenty minutes to sort themselves out.

Eddy stood by rink number one as Winnie the witch Wilson stood looking frail but determined as she read from her scorecard which she held in her wrinkled hand: 'Eddy Edmunds is my number one.' she read aloud, pointing a bony, yellowy finger directly at Eddy.

'My number one,' said the visiting Skip, Dan Dorkin, a short, round man with a bald head, beaming eyes and a large moustache, 'is Marlene Moss.' He pointed to Eddy's opposite number. Marlene had blonde hair cut short round her head, and wore thick, shovelled-on make up with thick red lipstick which stained her two front teeth, making them look pink.

'Hello there,' Eddy sprinted forward to introduce himself

to his opposite number, 'I'm Eddy-'

'I'm Marlene,' Marlene got in early, 'I don't really know the rules to bowling, this is my first season, so you'll have to excuse me if I don't know what to do.'

'But one of the many badges on your blazer says "Bowling at Wellerton for thirty years"', Eddy observed.

'Oh, no,' laughed Marlene with a sly look, 'it's not my badge, this is my first season, really.'

'That's just what I was going to say,' Eddy explained, 'this is *my* first season, too. In fact, this is my first real game, ever.'

'Oh yeah!' giggled Marlene accusingly, 'this is your first season. I've heard that old one before. You say it's your first game of your first season to make me think you're a novice, then smack a few touchers in, I know your game, mate.' Eddy gave up while the rest of the teams for the rinks were read out. Eddy's team consisted of: Eddy at number one, Evelyn "Two Cod" Brown, at number two, nicknamed for her love of all food, and lots of it, especially fish and chips, whose thick, dark hair was cut short over her pale face under round spectacles, and from the neck down, under her bowling outfit, was shaped like a barrel, thick, round and full, probably of fish and chips. At number three was Ron "Pulse" Dover, named after his insatiable lust for the ladies, no matter how old, infirm or frail, as long as they had a pulse, he tried his luck. Tall and grey haired with pale eyes peering over a long snooty nose and arrogant sneer, Pulse Dover was always smart, especially in his whites, and only had eyes for the girls.

The two Skips wandered to the far end of the rink, as their respective teams sorted themselves out, bringing their woods, drinks, chalk, measures and cardigans and waterproofs closer to their rink.

The opposing team on rink number one was the aforementioned Dan Dorkin as Skip, Marlene at number one and at number two and three were two elderly ladies, Joanny and Gina, who were the same in every way, clearly interchangeable. Both wore smart whites with pleated skirts, dark stockings and leather bowls shoes. Both wore thick make up and pinky lipstick, droopy sparkly earrings with matching bracelets on each wrist and sparkling rings on most fingers. Both ladies twisted their mouths into a half grin and held out a limp hand when introduced.

'It's visitors mat, and we're going straight off, no trial ends,' shouted Dan Dorkin from the other end of the rink, 'score of one on the first two ends.'

It was "visitors mat" so Marlene bowled first, watched anxiously by Eddy, hoping to see how much turn of the bias would be needed. Her back hand shot rolled gently down the left hand side of the rink and seemed to go on for ever, very, very slowly, finally coming to a stop next to the jack, accompanied by applause from the Wellerton team on rink one.

Now it was time for Eddy's first bowl in a real match. He felt his heart beating faster as he picked up his wood and stood on the mat. He bent low and let his wood go. It raced down the right hand side of the rink like a rocket. It raced past the jack, past the Skips and cracked! into the wood of the ditch. 'Just a bit heavy!' cried Witch Wilson as she angrily picked the wood up and put it in the tray on the flagstones at the end of the green. Eddy had never felt so bad.

When Marlene took her second shot it arrived just behind the jack, a good shot, in case the jack was knocked backwards, it would be waiting. As Eddy took his second shot, he tried so hard to hold back on the weight behind the bowl. This time he actually achieved less power, so much so that the bowl didn't get much further than half way down the rink. 'It's nearer to you than it is to us,' laughed Dan Dorkin. Eddy heard that remark for the first time in his life, but not the last time, and learned to hate it.

At last all six players had bowled their two woods, and Eddy joined them as they walked up to the other end of the rink. 'Hello, dahlin.' Ron "Pulse" Dover said to Marlene as they walked down the green.

'Drop dead, letch.' muttered Marlene as she marched on without slowing down or looking at Pulse.

Ron turned his nose up at Marlene's back, then noticed that the team in rink number two were also walking the same way as themselves. He noticed that one of the Wellerton team, a very large lady was waddling along just in front of him; he leaned over and squeezed her bum. 'Ooohh,' she cried without looking round, 'two pints please milkman.'

CHAPTER NINE

Now it was the turn of the Captains to bowl, and the teams stood behind the jack to see what would happen. Dan took to the mat first, bent low and sent a seemingly slow bowl down the rink which lazily oozed its way along and clunk! It whicked off one, then another wood to end close to the jack. Marlene whooped and clapped as the two bejewelled ladies' mouths twisted into smug grins.

Then Witch Wilson took her turn. She bent low, drew her arm back and whoosh! she rocketed the wood down the green. It zoomed into the head and smacked into the woods surrounding the jack with a tremendous thwack! All the surrounding players jumped up to let the woods fly in all directions, and the two bejewelled ladies positively jangled their jewellery as they landed back on the grass. 'Wow,' exclaimed Eddy as the dust settled, 'what's happened to the head now?'

They gathered round and saw that the shot that the Witch had fired had dislodged Wellerton's holding wood and replaced it with a BUMs. Now it was the turn of the home team to wear smug grins, including Eddy, and the Wellerton's faces had a vengeful, accusing look. Last two woods to come. Dan took careful aim and once again his wood seemed to sail serenely down the green like a smooth, silent electric ball, it calmly and gently slowed as it entered the head and nudged the Witch's bowl out of the way, then knocked a Wellerton wood nearer to the jack and the two stopped gracefully, one on either side of the jack.

Enraged, the Witch literally hurled her last wood at the head, if anything, even faster and more furious that the last time. The watching players round the head dived for cover as the wood raced down the green like an angry charging bull. This time the shot was wild and the wood slammed past the

34

head and hit the ditch with such a smack! that all the bowlers on the rest of the rinks looked round in shock. 'Missed the bugger!' cried the Witch.

'Oohh,' cried Marlene, 'we've got two! Holding two!' Marlene cried down the green to Dan.

'No you're not!' Evelyn "2 Cod" Brown insisted as she bullied Marlene out of the way with her large bulk.

'Yes we are!' bejewelled Joanny stamped forward, 'I'm the number two and I say we're holding two. Look! You can see we're holding two.' It was true, there were two Wellerton woods closest to the jack.

'Yes, you are holding two,' Ron Dover conceded, 'but the rules that were told to us was "one on the first two ends", so you can only have a score of one.'

'No!' cried Gina, 'he said "two on one", you can't cheat me.'

'Hurry up you lot!' Winnie Wilson screamed from the other end of the rink, 'It's one on the first two ends! Surely that's clear enough?' Scowling, Joanny turned over a "1" on the scoreboard, as Eddy gathered the woods up in the pusher. Eddy's first end, the very first time he had bowled in a competition had been a nightmare.

The game went on and all the rinks were full of shouts of encouragement and disappointment, "ohs" and "aaahhs" and "well you bowled" and "last wood shot". The bar was open, the drinks flowing, the laughter loud as the Skips enjoyed the opportunity to shout scorn, abuse, and the occasional piece of advice, good or bad, to their players. Passers by, outside the tall bushes of the bowling green, wondered what the hell was going on behind the green hedge.

Eddy looked over at the whole green and was amazed to see how the entire green was taken up with rolling woods, touchers, measures and woods in the ditch as players gave their all in the name of bowls.

In the rink number three, a whole rink away from Eddy, he could hear their Skip, Lilly Puddle, dishing advice to her players, 'That's right dear one behind the jack is always worth it more than I can say for my local supermarket the price of cucumbers today not like during the rationing and me back doors jammed an' I couldn't get to the snobs on Tuesday or was it Wednesday cos the bus was early or was my mantelpiece clock wrong.'

The game dragged on and each time Eddy's bowling seemed further to go wrong; either his wood went too wide or too narrow, and just after the second wood, when he reckoned that his next wood would be in between the two, and just about right, he didn't have another bowl until the next end, when it started all over again. It could not have been worse.

'Seven! We've got a Seven!' screeched Wellerton's Joanny on his rink, 'yes, it's a Seven to us!' Eddy peeked through the crowd standing by the head. It *was* a Seven to them. The two old girls insisted on counting it up twice, then doing it all again, this time carefully putting each wood on a nearby large cloth and counting loudly: 'One!' 'Two!' until all seven were counted out as loud as possible.

'Ahem. Ahem!' A loud false cough sounded in Eddy's ear.

'What's up?' Eddy twisted angrily around. It was the Ladies Captain, GG Glendenning, 'what *is* wrong now?'

'It's your shirt,' GG said haughtily, her bulging eyes glaring, 'it's not quite right. It looks a bit grey to me. It should be white, pure white like the rest of us. Your shirt isn't right. Not really white white. I could have you banned from the green for breach of green etiquette, not being properly dressed.'

'But it *is* white!' Eddy exploded, 'and what about him?' Eddy pointed to rink four, where another game was in play. There Kirkland Dunne was just bowling, bending low and slowly releasing his wood with a confident smile as he watched it ooze down the rink to roll to a stop against the jack. 'He isn't wearing white, even, it's red! He's wearing a red top! Why don't you ban him?'

'Weeelllll,' GG put on a sickly, goofy grin, 'it is a *bit* white...'

'A *bit* white!' raged Eddy, 'it's *red*! The only white on that T-shirt is the bold letters on the back telling the word he's the best bowler, ever. Surely, if you want to ban anyone, it's him!'

'Aahh,' smiled GG, 'he's Kirkland Dunne, he's our best player. If he loses a game he storms off. If we told him what to wear, we'd probably never see him again.'

CHAPTER TEN

Dave Sirly was doing great business at the bar, his head swimming as he swirled backwards and forwards serving many pints and glasses of wine, keeping his own beer mug full, swinging back and forth from bar to till. 'Dave! Dave!' a deep voice called. Dave swirled round, nearly spinning himself off his feet. His bleary eyes caught sight of a big red face as Horatio Anchor sped by the bar on his way to a very fast visit to the toilet, which was usually rushed so that the player could get back to the rink before his next bowl. Moments later he sped out again, this time on his way back. 'Four pints of the 'Ead banging strong stuff on rink five.' he shouted as he disappeared back onto the green.

Dave glumly nodded, he wasn't very keen on taking drinks out around the green, first of all he had to keep stopping every time he walked past a rink that was bowling towards him or risk getting shouted at by fussy self-important players who wanted everything to be still when they bowled. Then when he caught up with the people who had ordered drinks, they always forgot that they had ordered drinks on the green without paying first.

Dave grudgingly poured the four pints, put them on a tray and took himself and it out onto the paths surrounding the green. He weaved his way through the players and watchers until he was at rink five. 'Here we are then,' Dave announced loudly as he banged down the tray and began unloading pints of the strong lager. 'As ordered! Four pints!' Not one of the BUMs players looked round, all too intent on the game. Dave shrugged his shoulders and slumped back to the bar.

On rink six the players were examining the head after everyone had bowled. The number two's stepped into the head and looked closely. 'This one,' said the ancient lady of the Wellerton club, 'is nearest, and that's ours. And this one, that's second wood, is also ours.' She picked up the two woods and placed them on a rectangle of cloth she carried for cleaning her woods and for this reason; to keep winning woods separate. 'Now,' she continued, 'what's next?' She looked at the remainder of the head, leaning close.

'Well, theeshe c'n go,' said a small BUMs player, Cliff Gibbs, whose long brown hair was tied at the back of his head and who sported a droopy moustache, 'I reckon theseshe are in the way.' He picked up the next two nearest woods to the jack and threw them into the ditch.

'What are you doing?' demanded the Wellerton lady, 'they are the nearest woods to the jack. You can't move *them*! They're supposed to be measured next. And you're drunk!'

'Don' be daf', woman,' Cliff said with a crooked grin as he stepped back onto another wood and fell flat on his back.

On rink five, the Skip, Pricey Watergate was giving advice to his players as each took his or her turn to bowl. 'Now come this way Jason, to the left and swing in here.' Pricey stood immaculately dressed and presented as he stood over the head and pointed to where he wanted the next wood to go.

'What does he know?' grumbled the BUMs player, Jason "Scruffbag" Cable, 'I can't get a wood in that tiny gap. I know more about this game than he does. I been playing more years than he has. Who does he think he is? Oi! Pricey! I can't get in there! I'm going the other side!'

'Eh?' spluttered Pricey, cupping a hand round his ear, 'Oh! Well. I'm supposed to be giving you good advice from someone who's at the head and can see what's required to try and win this head.'

'What does he know?' grumbled Scruffbag, 'I been playing for twenty five years and he's been playing for ten minutes. Oi! Pricey! Mind your ankles!' Scruffbag bent his knee, stooped low and bowled a curving shot. The wood left his hand at a fast pace over on the left of the green. It snaked further over to the left, seeming to pick up speed. It sped even further to the left and before anyone could stop it or see it coming, it scored a direct hit on the jack – on the next rink, number four.

'Ye Gods!' Pricey shouted as he made a much-too-late dive for the wood, missing by a good ten feet.

'Perfect shot, that.' Scruffbag said in a satisfied way, as he lit a foul smelling cheroot. 'Perfect shot. Just got the wrong bias, that's all. An' I got a toucher.'

Back on rink one, Eddy began to feel really tired, he wasn't sure if it was because the game was for twenty one ends and it wasn't half way through yet or if he were tired because in this, his very first ever competitive game, and his team were being so badly and easily beaten.

Again it was his turn to bowl, after Marlene had bowled an unusual short shot; he trudged up to the mat, hardly took aim and let the shot go. 'Oh my God,' he thought, 'it's going so wide!' The wood careered down the right side of the rink, seeming to go wider and wider. But as it slowed down, it curved back in! It was slowing down, slower and slower, creeping nearer and nearer to the completely open jack. Nearer and nearer it rolled, and finally came to a rest one inch from the right side of the jack!

Open mouthed, Eddy couldn't believe he had just bowled such a fantastic shot! Camera! Did anyone have a camera? Please take a photo. The Wellerton team on rink one suddenly looked disgusted, while the BUMs team applauded and said all the things he had always wanted to hear since he had started bowling. 'Oh well bowled!' crowed Ron "Pulse" Dover, while at the other end of the rink Winnie Wilson raised her hands over her head and clapped.

'Don't worry,' smiled Marlene with a confident snigger, 'I'll soon get that wood out of the way.' Eddy stood stunned.

40

She wouldn't knock his lovely shot out of the way would she? Of course she would, it was the nature of the game! Eddy watched intently as Marlene stood on the mat to bowl. She crouched low, carefully judging bias, power and distance. Then she drew back her arm and bowled. The wood surged down the grass, smoothly driving in a perfect curve down the right. If the bias was correct, it would hit Eddy's wood spot on.

Marlene's wood sped on as if pulled by a powerful magnet, straight at Eddy's holding shot. Closer and closer it ran and judging by its speed, would knock out Eddy's shot and replace it with Marlene's. Eddy held his breath. The wood was only two feet away! It whistled passed Eddy's wood with only a millimetre to spare, coming to a stop about four feet behind the jack. Eddy still had shot wood! And now it was time for his second bowl.

He strode to the mat and stopped. What if he did the same shot again and this time knocked his own wood out of the way? They'd laugh at him. He'd look a fool. He decided to go for a back hand shot, changed bias on the wood in his hand and bowled, gently, oh so gently to the left. If this wood didn't get there at least he would still have shot wood. The wood sailed serenely down the left side of the rink, slowing down all the way. 'Well,' thought Eddy, 'if it don't get there, I'm still holding. Me!' Then the wood crossed some patchy brown grass – and speeded up! Eddy watch in horror as the slow wood picked up a bit of speed, and raced on, coming to a stop on the left side of the jack, only an inch or so away.

Eddy clinched his mouth tight shut, clenched his knuckles and squeezed his bum closed tighter, as well as his eyes in pure excitement! He was holding two! One wood on either side of the jack. To a loud applause from his team mates, Eddy gave a small salute, a quick bow, blushed, and proudly walked from the mat.

Next, bejewelled Joanny walked onto the mat, and threw

the wood down the green, it left her hand at waist height, and bounced onto the grass, Joanny took hardly a look. The wood sailed down the middle of the rink and took the jack from between Eddy's woods and rolled it and Joanny's wood into the ditch, leaving Eddy in deep, deep depression.

CHAPTER ELEVEN

The door from the dance floor of the club house swung open and Amy "Zon" Sirly pushed her way onto the seating area, sitting her bulk on a vacant seat while her assistant, Rene Bunnell, a small mouse-like young woman with dark, scruffy hair poked into a wire-like hair net, with her unclean-looking pallid skin and dark eyes over pinched nose and mouth, sat next to her in a wrap-round off-whitish cook's coat.

Amy had left the kitchen after just finishing browning the mince for the Shepherd's pie and emptied the very large pan into the casserole dish ready for the mashed potatoes to go on top. She had dropped the pan back onto the gas ring and flipped the gas tap switch to "Off" but her fingers had slipped and the gas stayed on full flame. All the little bits of mince and fat in the very large pan began to get hotter and hotter and crackle and spit...

'Fag time, Amy?' asked one or two of the BUMs players who knew her well, as she stepped outside.

'Yes dahlin'.' she answered with a smile and a flash of her large eyes and billowing breasts, 'fag break while the dinner's cooking.' From somewhere in the depths of her bosom she fished out a packet of cigarettes and a lighter, took one for herself and one for Rene; they lit up, puffing away, while behind her, following out from inside the club wafted a warm smell of meat being cooked.

'Who's winning?' Amyzon Sirly asked, not bothering to look at the scoreboards at the other end of the green.

'Don't ask.' came the reply that she had expected.

'Would you lovely ladies like a drink?' asked Ron Dover, the next time the BUMs team was at their end of the rink, as he beamed his leering, lusty eyes at Amyzon's heaving breasts.

'Ooh, yes, dahlin',' oozed Amyzon, 'two large gin and tonic's please!' She leaned forwards and gave Pulse Dover a full view down the front of her open white cooks coat. Pulse shivered from head to toe without taking his eyes away, then, grinning, ran into the club shouting: 'Dave! Dave! Two large gin and tonic's on rink one!'

'He's disgusting!' murmured the tiny Rene, as she watched Pulse run back to rink one, 'that's all he thinks of.'

'Yeah, I know, dahlin',' laughed Amyzon, 'one look down there has cost him two gin and tonic's, and that's as close as he's going to get.' The two cooking ladies giggled, and each time behind them the club door was opened, the warm smell of cooking food from the kitchen wafted out.

Tempers were flaring on rink four where Kirkland Dunne and a Wellerton player, Jay Donnell, a large round faced man with a full head of wild hair, full moustache and round belly. They stood toe to toe, or rather belly to belly. Opposing woods had been similar distances from the jack and had needed measuring.

'You couldn't measure woods with a tape measure!' Kirkland fumed.

'I been playing bowls since before you was born,' boomed Jay, 'if indeed you was born.' He pushed his immense belly forward into Kirkland. 'I measured it properly, and my wood's closer than yours.'

'It is now!' roared Kirkland, 'but my wood was closer until you bent down and hid us from view, then moved your wood with your belly!'

'Ooh,' said a Wellerton lady, a member of Jay Donnell's team, 'do they have to argue? What with that wonderful smell of cooking, let's just get it over with and eat.' By now, the warm, smell of cooking meat was covering the whole green and players were beginning to feel hungry.

Inside the clubhouse, the multitude of onlookers sat round the bar area sipping wine and spirits or gulping pints with faces turned towards the green outside, as they imagined how much better they would play if only they were on the green instead of the people making fools of themselves outside. Unnoticed around them, the warm, clinging smell of the cooking that wafted through the air was now a thin fog of smoke.

On rink three, the Skip, Lily "Lips" Puddle stood at the head and called down directions and advice to her team-mates, waving a small towel above the woods. 'That's right Sid, whick off here or there to wiggle in to the jack like I did in the fifties an' me phones still not working I'd tell 'em but I can't get through cos me phones not working an me butcher aint got pigs trotters no more.'

Lily looked down the rink at her team, who were waiting to bowl, and shook her head. She looked, then stared hard, and shook her head again. A dark smoke-like mist was gently rolling up the rink towards her and her opposing Skip John Beale, a small, thin, hairless little man whose white shirt and flannel trousers seemed to flap in the breeze as if there was no-one inside.

'Here, what's this?' John Beale asked, 'What's that smokey mist rolling towards us? I can't see our teams at the other end of the rink.'

'Well I don't know,' answered Lily, peering ahead, 'my husband had one of them when he got mad or was it a red mist but he liked page three girls then the lens fell out of me specs an I got on the wrong bus to the shops but they chucked me out at Gatwick Airport or it could be smoke.'

Back in the kitchen the extremely high gas flames under the glowing mince meat pan was now causing the burnt remains to spit flames and black smoke began to fill the club. In the club house the watchers had eyes only for the green, and hadn't noticed while the smoke poured out.

Bbrrrrrrrrrrrrrrring! A smoke alarm tripped in the kitchen ceiling. 'Oh, pooh!' cried Norbert Brown, husband of Evelyn "2 Cod" Brown, who raised his overfed bulk from an armchair, went into the electrics locker near the door and switched off the alarm, without taking his attention from the rinks outside.

The shiny red fire engine of the Morten Fire Brigade swung round the corner, blues and twos flashing and sirens blaring. The fire engine was forty five years old and had been made redundant by the London Fire Brigade many years ago, when it had been bought by the Morten Council and manned by volunteer squads of firefighters for the county of Cheswick.

The venerable machine roared along, passing cars and buses which reverently pulled out of the way for them to get to their emergency. People stopped on the pavements and watched as it raced by, answering an automatic call from Upper Morten bowling club.

In the front of the fire engine sat two men, pulling on their uniform tops and fire helmets as they drove. At the wheel was Bert Frimly, grizzled old campaigner who had served in the London Fire Brigade all his working life, and now as a retired man was in charge of Morten's volunteers. In years gone by, Bert had been known as "Flaming" Frimly, but now his remaining hair was thin and white, just like his stubbly beard. But there was a grin on Berts face as he drove as fast as possible; he loved to fight fires! Next to him was Billy Frimly, grandson of Bert. Tall and thin with short cropped red hair, red eyebrows and greenish eyes, face covered in teenage spots, Billy held on as the engine swerved around another corner.

'Oh no!' cried Bert, slamming on the brakes, bringing them to a shuddering stop, 'we can't get by! This stupid parking outside the bowling club has blocked the road.'

'Look! Granddad!' shouted Billy, 'there's a gap in the hedge to the club. We could take a hose through there.'

'Well done, Billy!' cried Bert, jamming the hand brake on and clambering out of the cab. 'Let's get out the hose!'

Soon they burst through the hedge onto the side of the

green and saw at the pavilion end the Skips and the other end of the rinks, the teams. They dashed towards the club house, Billy first, followed by Bert hauling along the hose. As Billy turned the corner of the green at the end of the rinks, a voice boomed: 'Oi! You there!' Billy and Bert stopped dead, and turned to see a crowd of men at the other end of the green. One of the men, bent low, holding a large black ball stood glaring at him. 'Stand still!' he continued, 'You can't walk in front of a bowler! Well! Where's the bowling green etiquette of the young people of today I ask you?'

'Get on, Billy!' cried Billy's Granddad Bert, dropping the hose and running forward, 'take no notice of him.'

'Hey! I say!' screamed a voice on the next rink the firemen passed. 'Stop still! I'm bowling!' The two firemen ignored the call and raced on into the clubhouse. Following the stream of smoke, they ran into the kitchen where Bert switched off the gas, and donning his thick gloves, swept the large pan from the oven top, and ran out of the back door with the red-glowing pan. Running to a rain water butt, Bert dowsed the red hot pan, which hissed and steamed until it was cooled, and then replaced it back in the kitchen on the oven top.

The firemen stood up and took a deep breath. Job done! At that moment Amyzon and her assistant returned to the kitchen and resumed cooking without noticing the firemen.

CHAPTER TWELVE

At last they bowled their last woods and Eddy was pleased for the first time in the game. He was unbelievably tired and irritable; he had played terribly and had received little encouragement from his own team-mates and nothing but off-hand, derogatory remarks from the grinning, smirking opposing team. And Bowls Upper Morton had lost so pathetically badly.

'Carry on like this, mate,' giggled the old hag Joanny, jangling her jewellery, 'and you'll definitely be last in the whole country, let alone Cheswick county!' The easily winning Wellerton team took up their woods, cardigans and general belongings and, congratulating themselves and laughing out loud with mocking looks at the BUMs players they slowly wandered back into the changing rooms and back to the bar in a jovial mood.

In the BUMs men's changing rooms, all was gloom 'You was all useless, 'cept me,' remarked Kirkland as he changed from his bright red T-shirt into another bright red T-shirt, 'but I've got this great idea on how to win the big fight against Pilkington for the bottom of the Cheswick bowling clubs next week.'

'You've got an idea we could win?' chorused all of the men as they changed out of their whites.

'Yeah, I have,' at least with my idea this club would stand a chance of winning,' said Kirkland picking up his woods and making for the door, 'the idea is this: You lot don't turn up at all. I'd have more chance of winning by playing on me own.' He opened the door and stalked out.

Outside, now that the players were going inside the club house, Jackson Irons trudged around collecting up the jacks, irons, mats and scoreboards mumbling to himself on the uselessness of such a badly lost game, while his eyes darted left and right hoping to catch someone trying to steal his job of collecting up the items left on the green. He stacked the goods away.

'Well, that didn't give us much hope for the game against Pilkington, did it?' Jason Cable asked Jackson Irons as he led the smaller man to the folded up tapes of the fence, dodging their way through the milling players, 'let's get that electrified fence up and get on with the dinner.'

From one corner Jason lifted the four strands of fence on its post and walked across the green to the other corner and fixed in the post while Jackson went to the opposite corner and did the same. Soon all of the green was surrounded by the four white strips of fencing.

At the same time, Aldous collared Old Nick Chambers. Aldous pulled at his coat and Old Nick followed, being marched along, his frantically pumping little legs poking out of the bottom of his white coat, his screwed up little face twisted, his little legs going nineteen to the dozen beneath his belly.

Then Aldous dragged Nick to the little alley between the changing rooms, where the little man was pushed and shoved down to the large rubber-covered metal handle, which was up in the "OFF" position. 'Now,' said Aldous, pointing first to Nick and next to the handle, 'when I say go, pull the handle down to turn the electrical fence on.'

'Eh? Wassat?' shouted Old Nick, 'what'd you say?'

'Listen, you old git!' cried Aldous, 'when I shout "GO", turn the handle down to turn it on.'

'When you say "GO"?' asked Nick.

Aldous turned back to the green to see if anyone was touching the fence as he replied, 'Yes, when I say "GO"!'

'Right,' said Old Nick and slammed the handle down into the "ON" position.

'Not yet, you idiot!' cried Aldous, 'I haven't had time to check if everyone's clear of the fence yet.' He peered fearfully round the corner of the changing room alley onto the green.

No one was lying on the green after being shocked by the fence. 'I said wait till I shout- Oh, what does it matter, you've done it now.' Aldous gave up and went back into the club house.

Inside the clubhouse, the tables, already laid out by the two helper ladies, the Blagett sisters, Dotty and Betty, had put on each of them a large pot upon which was painted a rink number and both opposing teams of the players sat around the table with the number of the rink they had played on, and sticking up from each of the pots were raffle tickets, enough raffle tickets for two for every person at each table. Amyzon Swirly and her assistant brought out plates and served up a slightly overcooked dinner for everyone. On the head table facing the rest of the lined up tables sat the two captains and their teams.

At table 2, Evelyn "2 Cod" Brown shoved back her thick spectacles and shovelled food from the serving plates onto her own, then shovelled it into her gaping mouth. When she had finished, she looked at the half eaten food on the persons plate on the opposite side and said, with a full mouth; 'you gonna eat that? I'll have it!'

While on table 3, Lily continued. 'Didn't do much did we like my back door its stuck and doesn't do much an' me radiator keeps hissing an' me hot plate wont get hot so I put sellotape on it but it still hisses then the man in the shop asked me if I wanted an Ipad I said no a new lens will do.'

Table 4 saw Kirkland Dunne moodily sipping brandy and not eating. 'My Gawd,' laughed Jay Donnell his large round face grinning, his wild hair still sticking out, his moustache covered in thick gravy as he filled his round belly, 'we certainly gave you lot a good hiding.'

'And how would *you* like a good hiding?' growled Kirkland his eyes narrowing dangerously.

On table 5 Pricey Watergate was noble in defeat. 'Yes,

I must say,' he announced to all at the table, 'I must say that you, Wellerton, as a team were magnificent, well done to you all.'

'Yeah,' agreed a grinning, bald youngish man on his table, 'and you Upper Morten players were rubbish.'

When the meal was over, the BUMs Captain stood to say a few words. 'Maidens and Gentiles,' began Mad Mick, 'Pizzas and flaming tissues to Wellington!' Mick beamed and sat down, as the bewildered assemblage of players wondered what he had just said, then applauded warmly.

'Well thank you for those lovely words,' said Wellerton Captain, Jerry Cann as he stood up. He ran a hand over his pointed head and smoothed back his stringy hair as his long bony nose flicked this way and that as he looked at his audience of diners through narrowed eyes. 'Well, that was fun, wasn't it? I mean, there's no need to look at the scores, it was a complete whitewash, and frankly, I really am looking forward to your game against Pilkington next week. Ha-ha!' Jerry sat down and laid his hands over his protruding round belly.

CHAPTER THIRTEEN

The meal was now nearing its end and Gladys Glendenning rose from her table and surveyed the numbered pots in the centre of each table. And yes, she noted, there were no raffle tickets sticking from the pots meaning that all the tickets had been sold. The money in the pots would go to the person who ran the raffle who would use it for the club. She brushed back her brown curly hair, and put on a toothy smile, then went to a table at the side of the diners and pulled towards her a random number chooser machine, which would show on a bright screen the winning numbers in tiny lighted-up figures.

'It's raffle time!' GG announced in a loud booming voice, 'who'll be a lucky winner today?'

'Who bloody cares?'

'Can't hear you!' came the usual replies.

'Sorry!' chirped GG, picking up a cordless microphone and switching it on. As she turned back to the diners, she took a quick look at the prizes. Two bottles of light wine, four cans of bitter, three packets of jelly babies, a pot plant, a cake and a bottle of Pound Shop shampoo. 'Well,' she continued, holding the mike to her lips, 'here … go. And the … number is … and thirty four. Anybody got … thirty four?'

'I've got thirty four!' beamed a man on one of the tables.

'I've got one hundred and thirty four!' cried a red-faced man.

'Is it two hundred and thirty four?' asked someone else.

'No,' said GG, 'it's … and thirty four … look … for you … like. Oh bugger! This mikes f… I think … up.' GG threw down the microphone and shouted: 'It's a hundred and thirty four!'

'That's me!' beamed the red-faced man again. He stood up and shuffled around the tables to the prizes, a grin on his roundish red face which was topped with dark brown hair. 'What prize shall I pick? Oh, I hope there's a holiday weekend as the first prize or a day at a theme park ... Oh, it's a couple of bottles of wine, cans of beer, and I don't drink.' He shuffled off with the shampoo.

Not long after, all the prizes had been won and taken away amid much cat-calling, laughing and mickey taking. By this time GG had found a different microphone which worked, and continued with her speech.

'I'd like to thank the ladies for cooking the meal and the volunteers for keeping the bar open,' she said, 'Now, the scores for today's game ... well, the score doesn't really matter does it, it was only a friendly game-'

'No! I wouldn't want to read out the scores if I was a BUMs player, either!' laughed a Wellerton man. The opposing team roared with laughter. 'There's no such thing as a friendly game, anyway.'

Eventually the dinner came to an end and the players left their seats and made for the bar or the changing rooms for their belongings and the trip home. Dotty and Betty Blagett took great sighs and trudged through the dropped peas and potatoes that littered the floor and began wiping the table-tops clean and then folding them up. 'It's dart night tomorrow,' Dotty said as she began to turn the tables upside down and fold the legs, 'so they won't need any tables out.'

'No,' said Betty, sliding on a dropped carrot, 'let's put them all away.' They laboured away at their never ending task.

At long last all the tables had been wiped, folded and stacked along one wall of the club as the ladies began to rack-up the chairs. No one else helped as they swept up the messy floor and took a dust pan and brush and cleared it all away.

In the kitchen, Amyzon Sirly and her helper Rene Bunnell threw piles of plates, cups and saucers, pots and pans, knives and forks and many kitchen utensils in the general direction of the sink, and left. 'Cooking's what I do,' smiled Amy, 'cleaning ups for the ladies committee.'

Watching the Blagett sisters clearing, cleaning and folding the tables, then stacking the chairs, Aldous Hiller snarled at the people sitting at his table: 'We look terrible. We're gonna be the two hundred and eightieth team in Cheswick unless we can pull something out of the blue and beat Pilkington.' Aldous scratched his stubbly chin as he glanced, one at a time at Horatio Anchor, Pricey Watergate and Fergus O'Brien, 'I mean, I must be able to do something about the last game of the season, to get us to win it by any means. I'm not for nothing the President of this club, the Honorary Secretary, the leader of the Bowls Upper Morten Limited Company, Entertainment Advisor, Beverage Manager and Financial Director of said bowls club. Convene the next meeting of The Allotments and Gardens Committee for a council of war.'

"Witch" Wilson marched by, her whispy white hair trailing behind her as she sped on, her wrinkled yellowish skin quivered as she strode purposefully forward. The red gash in her face which was her mouth opened wide as she spoke, 'Girls! Dotty! Betty! Have you forgotten? It's singing lessons tonight. You've got to leave one table out and four rows of chairs out!' She marched on.

'Oh pooh!' cried Betty

'Old Witch!' murmured Dotty.

'Then there's the washing up in the kitchen to do!' Winnie called back as she disappeared out of the club house.

CHAPTER FOURTEEN

Eddy sat in the smelly, dusty, clingy atmosphere of the men's changing room feeling down, so down, his first game had been a nightmare of failure and humiliation. 'Why so glum?' Ron "Pulse" Dover asked casually, as he admired himself in the faded mirror, 'we only lost a game. That's all.' He smoothed over his grey hair and posed this way and that, giving a handsome grin to himself, which actually came across as a sneer.

'I dunno,' sighed Eddy as he ran his hand down his neat, goatee beard, then bent to tie up his shoe laces, 'I mean, seriously, you've been playing for many years now, and I know you must have good days and bad days, but just how very bad was today in the general run of games of bowls?'

'Today was great, son,' Pulse gave a wicked wink and pursed his lips, 'great. Did you see the sheer size of that woman in the next rink to us? What a size! I'm taking her home later, if I can get her in my car! She's got her own pension and everything else is her own, except for the two big ones in front.'

'Two big ones in front!' Eddy stood back in horror, 'the two big ones in front are not her own? Do you mean-'

'Yeah! Teeth! I mean teeth,' laughed Pulse, 'the two big ones in front are a denture. She took them out to give me a kiss after the game. Nearly sucked me face in, I can tell you.' Eddy walked swiftly out of the changing room into the bar, hoping not to meet the large lady with the pension and two big false ones in front.

Standing at the bar gratefully sipping his pint, Eddy watched as the last people left the club after the game, some happily disappearing into the late afternoon sun, and some moaning about the bad performance of the BUMs players. Then Eddy's eyes fell on a table at the back of the bar area. President Aldous Hiller sat, his large belly standing like a small hill in his lap, his reddish brown eyes staring right at Eddy. Aldous lifted his arm and crooked a finger at Eddy, motioning him to come over. Eddy looked cautiously about himself. Was the club President crooking a finger at someone nearby? Or at him? Yes! He was beckoning him. 'What's old Adolf want, now?' mumbled Eddy to himself, as he wandered over to the table.

'Sit down Eddy,' commanded Aldous, 'I'd like to talk to you.' Eddy sat silently across the table from the heavyweight President.

'Look,' Eddy tried to explain, 'it was my first game on the green, I'm completely without experience-'

'No, no, no,' soothed Aldous, 'I know its a big moment for a new player, when they take part in their first game. No, no, what you need is a bit of experience, get some time in, so to speak. So I thought I'd put this your way.

'We have some home and away games against local bowls clubs, in a competition called The Raiders. We send three of our people to another club and they send three of their players here, for a game of triples. Then at the end of the season we have a tot up to see who's won the most games in this season. Raiders visit other clubs every other week that the series of games is held. Would you like to enter? We supply most of the transport, and tea and cakes are supplied by the clubs that are visited. What do you think?'

Eddy sat back, suddenly thoughtful. To represent his club! To go into other bowls clubs in his BUMs top. To be seen as a real bowler! Out there for his team! 'Hold on a minute!' Eddy abruptly cried. 'If you've got the likes of Kirkland Dunne and much more experienced players than I am, why are you asking me?'

'Kirkland on a Raiders game! He wouldn't be seen ...! ... I mean ... I'm asking you for that very reason, Eddy old boy,' smarmed Aldous, 'we'll send some experienced players with you, but you'll get the opportunity to gain some good quality learning time, at other venues, mixing with other players in a friendly contest in local clubs, that will welcome you along to their greens.'

'When is it?' asked Eddy, who was really enthusiastic about travelling to other clubs, to meet other players, see their club house, representing his own bowling club. It sounded like a good thing to do.

'Tomorrow,' answered Aldous, 'it's a two pee em start so better get here for twelve, for transportation. You're playing Little Middleton Fields.'

'I'll do it.' Eddy left the club with his head held high.

Next day, Eddy parked his little black two door car in the club car park at eleven forty five, and entered the club, wearing his white trousers and BUMs away game top, a white short-sleeved shirt with a blue circle over the top left pocket with the letters inside: BUM. He stood at the notice board where the cards for the forthcoming games and their teams were hung in rows, and searched each individual card. There! There it was! The card was headed: The Raiders, and below was stated the venue, Little Middleton Fields, and below the three names of the BUMs players had been filled in by Scruffbag Cable, then scribbled out and written in again, only to be filled in and scrubbed out again. But the first name had been re-written as Eddy Edmunds. That was right, it was himself. But who were the two names below? They had been scrubbed out so many times that the last names inserted were indecipherable.

Where were his two co-Raiders? Who were his two co-Raiders? Would it be Kirkland Dunne? Price Watergate? "Mad Mick" Fergus O'Brien? The club was empty of members, dark, unlit, and the bar wasn't open yet, although Eddy could hear the clinking of glasses or bottles somewhere around. Suddenly from below the bar, a head appeared. Dave Sirly's head.

Dave's watery eyes peered from an unshaven, grey-looking head. 'Mornin,' Dave greeted, through the mist of today's hangover, as he dragged himself up from his knees, 'just bottling up. What ja want? Pint? Not really open yet, but I'll pour you one if you want.'

'No, no thanks Dave,' Eddy whispered in the eerie silence of the bar, 'I'm on a Raiders away game today and I'm supposed to meet my fellow Raiders here but I can't see them anywhere.'

'Oh, that must be them, the only people in the club, they're sitting round the corner in the conservatory,' explained Dave, pointing to the glass roofed area. Eddy turned and strode towards the conservatory. Then just as he turned into the area he jumped back in shocked horror.

'Oh Gawd 'elp us!' he gulped, as he took just one look to see who his fellow Raiders were. Lily "Lips" Puddle and Nick "Nasty" Chambers! He peeped around the corner again. Lily was droning on, and on, while Nick sat and smiled a rat-like smile at her. Lily wore her usual blue club blazer over her white shirt and long wide skirt and blue bumpers. Nasty Nick sat with his full length white macintosh draped over his pot belly while his skinny little legs twitched back and forth below.

Eddy *had* to look round the corner again. He leaned over and held his head to one side, just one eye peering round. That one eye blinked. Something was wrong! What was it? Then he realised. Nick was smiling! It might have been a half-snigger, but it was a smile. How come? Most people, after sitting and listening to Lily began to lose the will to live, and here he was smiling. Eddy peeked again. Got it! Nick was smiling because he was as deaf as a post! He couldn't hear a word!

Eddy made a decision. He didn't like to let people down, but this was a special occasion. Sitting in the back of someone's car with these two all the way to Middleton Fields would be a fate worse than death. He'd tell them he was ill, tell them he'd twisted his ankle, tell them he'd been badly frightened by a pit pony, anything! He turned around and ran.

'Ooff!' Eddy slammed into a solid wall. He gasped, winded, as he saw that it wasn't a solid wall that he had ran into, it was Aldous Hiller's giant belly.

'Now, now, young Eddy,' snarled Aldous dangerously as he turned and pinned Eddy to the wall with his bulk, 'where'd you think you're going? You've got passengers in there waiting for you.'

'Well, I was just going-' Eddy stopped breathlessly, 'what do you mean, I've got passengers in there? You said transport would be supplied-'

'No, I didn't,' said Aldous pointing a wagging finger, 'I said we supply *most* of the transport, and of your Raiders team, *most* of them are round that corner awaiting for transport to be supplied – yours.' Aldous pulled Eddy round the corner by his neck and called to Lily and Nick. 'Come on, you two, Eddy's taking you to Middleton Fields.'

CHAPTER FIFTEEN

Eddy, Lily and Old Nick loaded their woods, gloves, wedges, cardigans and measures into the boot of Eddy's car. Then Nick slid into the back of the car, followed by Lily who had not stopped for breath. 'Course I played at Middleton Fields before when I was a conductress on the old trams an me custard pie fell down the back of the radiator but they use day tickets now so I scooped it out with a ruler an I had to leave me job at the Samaritans after you know, the suicides-'

'I can't do it!' Eddy pressed his hands to his ears and stood by the car in hopeless dejection, 'I can't take that non-stop jabber!'.

'Now don't be silly,' said Aldous, taking a small plastic oblong object from his own pocket and stuffing it into Eddy's top pocket. Attached to the little object were two tiny wires with earplugs which Aldous jammed into Eddy's ears. Music burst into Eddy's head! A radio! Eddy smiled gratefully at the big man and climbed into the car.

Eddy turned the wheel and the little car slowly moved on out of the club car park, as Aldous waved them off with a wicked grin. Suddenly the car skidded to a halt as Eddy slammed on the brakes. Eddy wound down the window and turned towards Aldous. 'Now what's wrong?' muttered Aldous.

'How do I get to Middleton?' groaned Eddy, appealing to the club President as he pulled out the earplugs.

'Oh, that's easy,' laughed the Pres, 'turn left out of the club, right at The Red Lion, straight passed The King's Head, left at The Rising Sun and look for the entrance to the bowling club on your left.' The little car bounced out of the car park and turned left as Eddy re-plugged himself into the radio.

Eddy drove on, looking for The Red Lion, occasionally looking into his mirror at the two in the back seat. Lily was still going on, he could see her slack mouth opening and closing like perpetual motion. Old Nick sat with his mouth and eyebrows trying to meet in the middle of his face as he glared out of the window. At The Red Lion Eddy turned right and looked for The King's Head, where he should turn left, or was it left at The Rising Sun. 'Oh God,' he said to himself, 'I've forgot.'

They drove on, and on, down seemingly endless streets, all lined with pubs, none of which was The Rising Sun or The King's Head. Eddy speeded up, he had to be aware of the passing time, and he was panicking. Then suddenly he saw a tiny sign by the entrance to a dirt alley: Middleton Bowling Club. Private Property. No Parking. Eddy smiled in relief as they turned in and drove down the bush-lined track.

They bumped down the muddy track, where they could see the top of a large hut behind the hedge, so Eddy drove on a bit until he came to a gate. They got out of the car and, taking their belongings with them tramped through the muddy grass towards the hut. A railing around the scruffy, unpainted old hut led to the main door, which had a faded sign above announcing: Middleton Club Members Only. They marched in.

'Blimey!' cried Old Nick, dumping his belongings onto a nearby table, 'it's even more broken down than BUMs.' They surveyed the peeling paint on the wooden walls, the faded notes on the notice board, the rickety furniture.

An unnoticed hatch in the wall was suddenly flung open and a man's red face appeared. The red face was surrounded by red hair and a red moustache and beard, as red eyebrows arched in question over reddish eyes. 'Ullo. What can I do for you?'

'Ahh,' said Eddy, pulling the earplugs from his ears, 'we're here-'

'Three teas and a scone, please,' Lily leaned forward.

'Eh? Whassat?' piped up Old Nick, 'Egg and chips for me.'

'No! Wait!' Eddy cried, 'let's just check, first.'

'Well,' smiled the red face in the serving hatch, 'I can make you a cuppa tea if you want one, but scones and egg and chips, I don't think so. But there's a cafe down the road-'

'Noo,' said Eddy, looking out of the dusty window, 'there's something wrong here, there's no one about and I can't see the green. Look, we're here for the game, the Raiders game. This is Middleton Bowls Club isn't it?'

'Yes ... well no,' said the serving hatch man, 'it was the Middleton Bowls club, but ten years ago it was sold to my boss Farmer Goldsmith, he keeps his farm equipment here, and I use this old hut as a changing room, but Goldsmith parks his tractor in the driveway. So, if I was you I'd get off his land pretty quick, 'cos he's a belligerent old sod who don't like people parking here, if he parks behind you, he'll block you in and you'll have to wait till he goes out tomorrow before you can get your car out.'

'OK,' sighed Eddy, herding his two passengers towards the door and dragging their belongings with him, 'we've got a Raiders game at Middleton, and I thought this place was it.'

'Oh, you don't want Middleton BC. No, no, you must mean *Little* Middleton BC. That's Little Middleton over there,' he said as he pointed to the dusty window of the hut. Eddy ran to the misty window, scrubbed his hand over the dirt and peered out. Across the other side of the overgrown field outside, at the very far end Eddy could see yet another large hut.

'Is *that* it?' asked Eddy, 'it that Little Middleton Bowls Club?'

'Oh yes,' smiled the man in the serving hatch.

'How do I get there?' Eddy pleaded.

'Well,' said the red faced one, 'you could drive straight over the field, that'd put you right in the car park of Little Middleton Bowls Club. But it would be a bit bouncy and muddy. Or you could turn round in the lane outside, go to the end, turn right into the road, turn right at the traffic lights and next right into the lane that leads to the Middleton club house. But you'll have to do it quick, mind, 'cos Farmer Goldsmith parks his tractor in that lane, and he won't move for anybody. Not on his own land he wont.'

'When's he due back?' Eddy asked in a sudden panic.

'Now.'

Eddy dragged Lily and Nick out of the shambles of a hut and ran to his car pulling them behind him struggling to hold on to their belongings. As she ran, Lily said between dragged steps: 'I – ran - like - this - once - to – get – the – tram – home – but – it - was – the – Eurostar-'

'Are – we – getting - some – tea – and - cake?' Nick blurted out between hurried pumping strides of his little legs.

Eddy pushed his charges into the back of the car and dived into the drivers seat. Starting up the motor, he jammed it into reverse and roared backwards. Then for the first time he looked into his rear view mirror. All he could see was a giant red tractor. It took up the width of the lane, its enormous tyres brushing the hedges on either side. 'Oh Gawd!' cried Eddy as he slammed on the brakes and they skidded to a dusty halt; his bad luck had turned to worse luck. What could he do?

A big man opened the door of the tractor and stepped down. He wore a green woolly hat, green jumper and brown trousers tucked into Wellington boots. His ruddy complexion seemed to glow as he turned to Eddy with a vicious sneer as he pointed to the sign post at the end of the lane. 'Private Property!' the Farmer roared, 'No Parking!' He turned and stamped off.

He couldn't get past the big red tractor. It was so bloody frustrating! And all he wanted to do was get to the hut at the other end of the field, for goodness sake! He could see it! There! Across the field! That was when he made up his mind. He'd catch up on time! He'd go straight ahead. 'Buckle up, people!' he shouted to his passengers as he selected first gear.

'A cheese sandwich will do.' Nick said as he settled down.

'The Eiffel Tower was nice though,' Lily said. Eddy jammed in the earplugs, stood on the accelerator and the little car bounced onto the mud.

Bang! Bang! There were some woods on the loose in the boot as the little car bounced over the ruts of soft mud, slinging up black, sticky streaks of slimy turf to the front and sides of the car as Eddy started the windscreen wipers and washers at the same time. They bounced along like a motorised yo-yo, getting covered in grass and mud. Once or twice Eddy glanced in the mirror. Old Nick's little legs were facing up to the roof of the car, while Lily hung on to her seat belt with both hands as she calmly continued to jabber as the speeding little car bounced across the field.

At last they came to a stop as the muddy vehicle slurred into the car park at the end of the field. Eddy cut the engine. It was getting so late! He opened the mud splattered door and left his two passengers to untangle themselves.

At last it was making sense. The large hut was freshly painted white, and people in their whites were sitting on the huts terraces drinking beer and tea, ready for their afternoon's game. The rinks looked a perfect smooth green and jacks and irons were being laid out. A youngish, dark haired man at one of the veranda tables hailed them as Old Nick and Lily dragged themselves from the mud-covered car and began to stagger to the door of the hut. 'Welcome,' said the man at the table, 'welcome to Little Middleton.'

'We made it,' sobbed Eddy, as the three shambled past the well-wisher towards the bar, 'we're here for the Raiders game, we went to Middleton at first.'

'Oh, I see,' smiled the man, 'your from the visiting Raiders team are you, the Buckland Bowlers.'

'No. We're from BUMs.' Eddy felt a great weariness overcome his body, 'no, we're not from Bucklands.'

'You're from BUMs?' laughed the sickeningly friendly man. 'BUMs are not playing here. No, no. You don't want Little Middleton; no, no, what you want is Little Middleton *Fields*.'

'Oh no,' groaned Eddy as he grabbed his retreating team-mates by the scruff of their necks, 'how the f-, I mean, how the heck do I get to Little Middleton Fields?'

'Well,' said the evil one, leaning back in his easy chair and taking just a small sip of his ice cool drink, 'you drive out of the car park, down the end of the lane; turn left and left again along the main road. Or there is a quicker way.'

'What is it?' Eddy pleaded.

'See that hut at the other side of these overgrown fields...' he said with a grin.

CHAPTER SIXTEEN

The battered little car, covered in mud crashed onto the car park from the field. It slewed around on slippery, mud-covered tyres and came to a rest in front of a crowd of white attired men and women, who were sipping drinks on the veranda of a pretty, white and green painted club house.

'Is this Little Middleton Fields?' Eddy shouted at the startled onlookers as his passengers burst from the other side of the muddy car.

'Yes, it is,' answered a tall, thin lady on the veranda, with a smile, 'and you must be the away team from BUMs. Hello.' Then she stood back in astonishment as Old Nick and Lily emerged from the other side of the car. After the ride over two mud covered fields, Lily's hair stood out as if electrified and Nick's long white macintosh had somehow got wrapped up in his legs as he staggered around trying to untangle himself from the tails of his coat.

'Three teas and a scone, please,' Lily rambled on as she picked her belongings from the mess in the boot and marched into the club house to find the changing rooms, 'an I'm seeing Ginny later to tell her about my operation, it straightened my eyes out but left me with really noisy wind.'

'It's a disgrace!' Old Nick blurted as he took his gear and marched into the club house, his little legs at last back to their normal double quick march, 'the bar's not open and there's no chips.'

After changing and reappearing on the green, the three BUMs players met their opponents for the Raiders game. Eddy was sweating; after the journey here, he had the feeling that things would go badly wrong. He looked at the opposing team. The three were all young men, all aggressively swift and strong looking, fit and healthy. And he had Lily and Nick.

'Welcome, you BUMs,' said their Skip Harry, a young

dark haired man with eyebrows that met in the middle above his stubby nose and firm-set mouth. In green club shirt and white trousers, his athletic body looked sleek and strong. 'I'm the Skip and here's my team. My number one is Ernie,' Ernie stepped forward. He was squat and muscular, like a wrestler, with a shaven skull over a rounded face with staring eyes and scowling mouth, dressed in his team's colours, he shook Eddy's hand in a vice-like grip. Eddy winced and then held his hand behind his back to try to get some feeling into it and check for broken bones.

'This is my number two: Steve.' Harry introduced a young man whose body builders rippling physique could not be hidden in his club uniform, with sparkling teeth, blond hair swept back over his head, his flashing blue eyes looking down in sympathy at Nick. Nick looked up at Steve, his head going back further and further as he looked at the tall figure before him.

'Ow de do dee,' Steve said in a quaint countryside accent, 'we'll 'ave a gret game if'n we gerrt t' chance.'

At last the game started and Eddy took his place on the mat for the first time, aware of the large crowd of watchers behind him on the veranda's of the club. Eddy took careful aim, bent his knee, got low, drew his arm back- 'Ahem!' A loud cough in Eddy's ear made him stumble forward with a jerk. He twisted round and stared at the two powerfully built men of the opposing team. Both stared back with set, serious but innocent looking faces.

Eddy turned back to the mat, took careful aim, bent his knee, got low, drew his arm back- Crack! Eddy jumped forward and dropped the wood as the loud crashing sound exploded behind him as a wood had been dropped onto another wood. Eddy picked up his wood and gave accusing stares at the two Little Middleton Fields players. Then he picked up his wood and bowled. As soon as the wood left his hand he knew he had been well and truly put off. The wood didn't get three quarters of the way there. 'Can't you get it up?' Skip Harry laughed, 'it's nearer to you than it is to us!' The crowd on the veranda's roared with laughter. Eddy turned red-faced in anger and embarrassment. That phrase again! Nearer to you!

Ernie bent his powerful, chunky body over the mat and bowled. His wood came to rest just in front of the left side of the jack. The Skips clapped. Eddy stood on the mat, took careful aim, bent his knee, got low, drew his arm back- 'Ahem!' This time Eddy ignored the noise and his wood rolled down the rink and stopped just behind the jack. Good shot! Ernie bowled again and this time his wood stopped just in front of his first wood.

Eddy took his third shot which he had aimed at breaking up the cluster of opposition woods at the left of the jack but his wood just flew by into the gutter.

Ernie took his third shot and left a cluster of woods on the left of the jack. Old Nick took the mat. 'That's right Nick,' shouted Lily, 'come on the right side and rest on the jack I could do with a rest meself-'

Old Nick took aim and drew back his arm- 'Ahem!' The loud cough exploded in his ear, Crack! The wood was dropped onto woods. Nick never jumped or showed surprise, he just serenely rolled his wood down the green till it stopped at the right hand side of the jack. Eddy wondered how Nick had not been put off by the obvious barracking, what nerves of steel Nick must have, he thought, until he realised: of course, Nick couldn't hear a thing!

Steve took his shot next which ended up behind the jack on the left next to Eddy's wood. Now Nick had his next shot. 'That's right Nick come on the right again same as before.' Lily cried.

'Eh? Wha she say?' Nick said as he picked up his last wood.

'She sayin' "Bowl to the left", Steve spoke into Nick's ear.

'No, she didn't!' Eddy cried, 'she said *right!*' Eddy was furious. But it was too late. Nick bowled to the left and his wood stopped on the left of Ernie's woods.

Steve took his third shot which went wide.

Nick took his third shot which followed Steve's.

Now it was the turn of the Skips and the teams walked to the other end of the rink, looking at the head as they went. 'I dunno why you went on the other side to what I told you, Nick.' Lily said in passing, 'still, we're still holding one.'

'Nick couldn't hear you,' ranted Eddy, 'but they told him the wrong side!' No one seemed to notice. Lily took her first shot and her wood stopped on the right of Nicks wood. 'We're holding two!' murmured Eddy. This wonderful condition lasted until Harry took his first bowl and speeding on the right it thwacked! smartly into Lily's wood and then Nick's wood knocking them into the jack which caused it to roll gently over to Ernie's woods on the left. The last few woods just surrounded the head as it was. The Little Middleton Fields team had won the first end.

Then they won the next end and most of the ends, except for a few when BUMs got the occasional score of one. 'At last,' thought Eddy, 'the last end. I'm really fed up.' He'd had to collect up the woods after each head and push them back near the gutter with the pusher, and only twice did he get the opportunity to bowl first.

'We'll have a measure on that.' Nick demanded, staring at the woods. Steve bent down and put his measure against the jack, slid out the flexible tape and held it to a Middleton wood. Next he did the same for a BUMs wood. 'We're closer!' cried Nick. Steve re-measured. This time when he slid out the measure for the BUMs wood, he turned the measure to one side first.

'No.' he stated, 'Middleton wood is closest.'

'No it isn't!' Eddy raged, 'you moved the measure!'

'Is thee callin' me a cheat?' Steve said dangerously.

'Erm …' Eddy gulped, he didn't start playing bowls for this. 'Well, yes,' he sputtered.

'An' rightly so,' interrupted Old Nick, angrily, 'he always cheats. But don't make a rumpus over it Eddy, we're losing 42-2 anyway'. He slapped Steve hard on the arm, then threw his hands up, boxing style, while his little legs danced a jig in a parody of Muhammed Ali's "shuffle".

Eddy couldn't wait to go home.

CHAPTER SEVENTEEN

The next day the Allotments and Gardens Committee sat yet again. Presiding as usual was Aldous Hiller, while around the table sat Secretary Captain Horatio Anchor, club Treasurer Price Watergate and Men's Bowls Captain Fergus O'Brien, all sipping large drinks. 'Now here's the thing, boys,' slurped Aldous over his gin and tonic, 'it's the big one this weekend. We're either two hundred and eightieth, or just for once two hundred and seventy ninth, and Pilkington go bottom. That is precisely what we want. Just no BUMs at the bottom of the league table.'

'If only we could just for once not be last,' mourned Pricey, 'if only BUMs weren't on the bottom.'

'Hysterectomy bubble and squeak!' Mad Mick agreed.

'If only we had a plan,' Horatio mused, 'to annihilate the opposition, kill 'em all stone dead.'

'I think I have that plan,' whispered Aldous out of the corner of his mouth, 'that new bloke Eddy, has just been on a Raiders away game, and then he came in here and moaned about it. The opposition fielded a team of young, eager, fit young men and they kicked ass ... well, BUMs actually.'

'And this gave you a plan?' Horatio asked.

'Yes, it did,' Aldous said with a wink, 'the final game of the season, our match with Pilkington is at the weekend. We'll do to Pilkington what Little Middleton Fields did to us. We'll get all our young men who can't play during the week because they're still working, and get them to play in the grand final for us. We'll field a superteam of young bloods.'

'But are they that good?' asked Pricey, 'I know that they play at night or at the weekend, so I don't actually see them very much, I imagine that they're dead keen but are they any good?'

'Well, I've picked out three here, all young, fit, good

players, who because of work can only play at the weekends or evenings, and just stand in the bar on Sundays,' said Aldous, 'the first is the young Danny Mallet-'

'Danny Mallet!' exploded Horatio, 'he's the builder chap isn't he? The loud mouth who usually plays well until he's drunk and can't stop shouting advice at everyone, even the more experienced players'.

'Yes, but he's a good player,' answered Aldous, 'his Dad taught him everything, and his Dad's a champion bowler.'

'Yes, I know,' pleaded Horatio, 'but his Dad's always drunk as well.'

'We'll cut down the flow of his booze on the day,' Aldous defended, 'and next I've picked Jermain Jones.'

'Now that boy *can* play bowls,' Pricey said, 'but he seems to suffer from a serious attention problem; he seems to forget himself, and he's got terrible shakes, he's always flicking his arms and legs in some sort of spasm.'

'That's because he's always listening to some sort of crazy music on his headphones,' Aldous replied, 'we'll confiscate them. And the next one I've picked is Kenny Layton-'

'Kin'a hate 'em.' Mad Mick snarled.

'No. Kenny's alright,' defended Aldous, wondering what Fergus had said, 'he's a good player, but he's a window cleaner and spends his time staring into people's houses and can't stop nosing.'

'And you think these young bloods will be able to beat the old boys of Pilkington?' asked Pricey, 'then who else will be on their team? You've only mentioned three players yet.'

'Yes,' sneered Aldous with a wink, 'if we confront the players of Pilkington with four new boys, they'll cotton on to the fact that we're up to something, they'll think we've imported a team from somewhere else, so we'll put our new boy Eddy Edmunds with them. Although Eddy's new here himself, he's quite well known as he trained in another club, and he's not a good player, so we'll put him in at number one, he'll look average enough to conceal our superteam.'

'But how come he'll be part of a superteam when he's not that good a bowler?' enquired Horatio.

'Because the number one's woods usually get knocked out of the way anyway.' Aldous grinned a crafty grin.

'But what if we lose on the rest of the rinks?' asked Pricey, 'and let's face it, we usually do.'

'Yes, I know,' Aldous held a finger to his nose, 'but if we do average on the other rinks and score a massive hit with the superteam, we'll win on points.'

'How do we know that they can all make it to this Sunday afternoon's game?' Pricey asked with a frown.

'Already called them on the phone,' smiled Aldous with a sly grin, 'and I've invited them to a roll up on Friday evening. All I've got to do now is to call Eddy Edmunds and tell him he's been picked for the showdown game against Pilkington as number one. Dave! Dave! Another round here for the Allotments and Gardens Committee. It's Horatio's turn for the first free drink.'

Eddy Edmunds couldn't believe what he was hearing from his telephone as he sat in his cosy front room. His wife Juney, in her comfortable cardigan and slacks looked concerned as she tried to hand him a cup of tea. 'But. But. I can't believe it,' Eddy said, his voice nearly hysterical, 'I had a disaster on the Raider's match and now you say I've been picked as number one for one of the teams against Pilkington?'

'That's right son,' droned Aldous with a bored sigh. 'Yeah, you had some bad times, but it's all good experience. And you're very popular with the rest of the players, and they know talent when they see it. So you're in. Come in on Friday evening for a roll up practice and meet your team-mates. I've taken into account what you told me about your opponents at the Raiders match and I've got you a team of young men! All too busy to play during the week because of work, so, when you play Pilkington on Sunday, you'll be the 'A' team!' Aldous put down the telephone receiver and pointed a finger towards his open mouth and pretended to be sick.

'They've picked me! Picked *me*!' Eddie said to the dead phone as he ran a hand over his neat grey moustache and goatee beard and grinned a wide grin. 'I'm to be the number one on the 'A' team! Eddy rolled a pretend wood along the thick front room carpet and stood thoughtfully as he watched his imaginary bowl ooze along the carpet into a distant rink where it came to rest on the jack. Then he rolled another imaginary wood and stood in splendour as it also rested on the other side of the wood. Then Eddy nonchalantly waved to the cheering imaginary crowd.

'Roll on, Sunday,' Eddy said, full of confidence, 'and roll up Friday!'

CHAPTER EIGHTEEN

Friday evening arrived and found Eddy at the BUM's club early, sipping a pint, eagerly awaiting the arrival of the superteam. At the back of the club the Blagett sisters were unfolding tables and positioning them out in preparation for the bingo and raffle that were held on alternate weeks to the knitting club. They pulled out the tables, unfolded legs, twisted the table over and placed it in position, puffing and blowing with the effort. Eddy still waited and waited, sitting alone. Where were the young men of his team?

A young man slouched into the club house bar. He was tall and thin with short cut dark hair, accusing dark eyes and eyebrows, a thin nose and unshaven chin. He wore a torn T-shirt and paint-daubed jeans with holes in the knees, and scruffy trainers. He ordered a pint from Dave and tipped it down his throat, glugging away until it was almost gone before blasting a really loud belch with his mouth fully open. 'Wotcha mate,' he said to Eddy with a smack of his lips, 'you Eddy Edmunds?'

'Yes ...' Eddy responded, wondering what was next.

'I'm Danny Mallet,' the young man said, proffering his right hand. Eddy shook the thin hand, noting the dried paint on the palm. Danny finished off his pint, ordered another and moved along the bar to Eddy's side. 'I wonder where the other two are ... oh, here they come.'

The club door opened and two young men entered. The first was a pale skinned young man, short and powerfully built with dark hair in ringlets. His dark eyes were raised to the ceiling as he jiggled his head around showing a blunt nose and white, even teeth. He wore a torn black T-shirt and rumpled blue jeans with old black, lace-up boots. 'Heyyaa, me man!' he cried as he high fived Danny, 'Aahhm Jermain,' he sung at Eddy as his head bobbed to the music in his ears. He accepted a pint from Dave and bobbed about into the club house.

Next a tall, mysterious looking young man followed, moodily looking around with intent brown eyes under a shaven head. He was tall with haunted looking eyes, beaky nose and full beard. He wore a flowery short-sleeved shirt over blue trousers and shabby trainers. 'You Eddy? I'm Kenny, the winders could do wiv a clean.' He passed moodily into the club after taking a beer from Dave.

'This is my superteam?' Eddy wondered to himself as he ventured out onto rink four for the roll up after changing into greys. Soon the three members of his working team emerged from the club house wearing the same clothes that they had arrived in but were now sporting decent bowling shoes and carrying their woods. 'Erm, I'm only just making a point lads,' Eddy gingerly said, 'but aren't we supposed to wear white top and grey trousers even though it's only a roll up?' The three stared back at Eddy without a sound, though Jermain still bobbed. 'Oh,' Eddy's voice trailed off, the three didn't seem to understand what he had just said.

Jermain skipped off up to the other end of the rink jerking little dance movements with arms and legs as he went. 'Oh well,' muttered Eddy, 'here we go.' He bowled up a jack which Jermain centred. Now Eddy took to the mat with his first wood. He bent low, drew back his arm and let the wood go with a flow.

The wood purred along the green as the back hand shot rolled gently up to the jack, stopping one inch away on the left side. 'Wow!' thought Eddy in surprise, 'what a great shot!'

'Bet you couldn't do that again!' Danny laughed, 'go on! It's only a roll up. Give it a try!' Eddy took to the mat again.

'OK,' he said with a laugh, 'this time I'll try a forehand shot.' He bent low and rolled the wood to the right. Away the wood oozed, in a curve on the right of the rink. It seemed to go too wide then turned left and stopped one inch away from the jack on the right. Eddy stood proudly back.

Kenny Layton stared gloomily at Eddy, 'I'm going to hit the middle of your two woods, knocking them out of the way, leaving mine as shot wood.' he murmured morosely. Kenny casually leaned from the mat and, hardly seeming to put any effort behind it at all, smoothly rolled the wood away. The rolling bowl sped down the rink and hit smack in the middle of Eddy's two woods knocking them away to left and right, the sudden impact of hitting the two woods stopped Kenny's wood which slowed to a gentle stop on the right of the jack. Fantastic!

Before anyone could react, Kenny leashed off a back hand shot which stopped at the right of the jack. Fantastic again! So Kenny's woods had moved Eddy's bowls from either side of the jack and replaced them with his own.

With a laugh Danny Mallet shot two woods one after the other, in fact there were his two woods on the rink at the same time. His woods knocked Kenny's woods out of the way and replaced them with his own. Eddy was speechless!

Jermain skipped down from the other side of the rink, still bobbing to the music in his ears, where he was met by Kenny who was holding three pints in his hands. The three took long gulps of the pints. 'Erm ... I say chaps,' Eddy ventured, 'just a thought. We're not allowed to take glasses onto the green are we?' The three stared at him quizzically as if he had spoken in a foreign language, then silently continued to drink.

Jermain took to the mat next and bowled a fast back hand. The wood whizzed down the green and slammed into Danny's woods, knocking them away and leaving his wood rolling with the jack. The jack rolled into the gulley, while Jermain's wood stopped just on the lip of the green above it. His next wood stopped next to his first wood on the lip of the green above the jack. 'Unbelievable!' burst Eddy, 'we really will be a superteam.'

After such a great roll up with his new - and he had to

admit it to himself - very strange team-mates, Eddy changed his clothes and left his woods in his locker, then, he passed the notice board on his way out and saw the list of names for the big game against Pilkington on Sunday. He almost gasped when he saw the list. There would be six rinks in use on that day, and it seemed as if a lot of the members of the club had put their name with Eddy's own, on the card for that game, and Jason Cable had written below: ALL PLAY. This was great!

At the back of the club the Blagett sisters were in deep negotiations with the wrinkled Winnie Wilson, who shook a yellowed and flappy-skinned finger at the sisters while trying to explain the meaning of the words "bingo" and "alternative Fridays", as tonight was Knitting club, and no tables were required, but two rows of forward facing chairs would be appreciated for the knitters and sewing crowd.

CHAPTER NINETEEN

Later that evening Eddy entered the club yet again, this time just for a relaxing pint and to idly watch the ladies' sewing and knitting evening, now that he looked forward to a good practice session of bowling on the next day, Saturday, which he had been told would be a good time for all those who could attend to roll up and get ready for the big one on Sunday with Pilkington.

Eddy sat with his pint at an empty table in the club seating area and noted a small commotion at the far end. The Blagett sisters were having a heated argument with Lady's Captain Gladys Glendenning, whose make-up free face was getting redder by the moment, as she made a point to the sisters, her Tweed jacket open, her thick, hairy legs splayed out beneath the tweed skirt. 'But you must know the difference,' GG stormed, 'it's tonight for the bingo, it's not bridge and cribbage card night or knitting! Everybody knows it's bingo tonight.'

'Oh pooh!' said the sisters together, 'Winnie Wilson moaned at us last night and said it was knitting night tonight.'

'What does Winnie the witch know about anything?' GG ranted, 'anyway, it's bingo tonight, so it's only one long table out front here on the dance floor and one small table for raffle tickets and quiz.'

'Oh pooh!' said the sisters together again and started moving and folding tables and chairs for the coming bingo session.

The club began to fill up as bowling players and social members came in to claim their usual seats at their usual tables, and greeted each other with hand shakes and kisses for the opposite sex, as though they hadn't seen each other for years, although they had last met yesterday in this very club.

Soon the club settled down to a busy buzz with Dave and Amy serving drinks over the bar as people sat and talked while over in the dance floor area, a tall smart, grey haired man checked out the microphone and number finder equipment for him to call out bingo numbers, Ron Dover's pale eyes peered over his snooty nose with an arrogant sneer at the ladies' in the club.

There were many new faces to Eddy's eyes, some he knew, were only at BUM's club for the social gatherings, although many he recognised. Over in the glassed roofed area Fergus O'Brien was giving someone the benefit of his vast experience. 'Pork pie and mash for Parliament death squad,' he informed a polite couple who had only dropped in for the bingo.

At a table in the seating area of the club Lily continued to talk to an audience of old ladies, who's eyes had began to glass over. 'Well doctor, I said, you can't bury me,' she droned, 'cos I was only asleep an they said I was inter continent but I'd stepped in the cat litter-' Eddy was only too pleased this time to be seated at the bar and just watching the members of the club interact.

The place was really getting busy now, raffle tickets were being sold at the same time as bingo cards and lucky number lotteries, and names were being put on the list of players required for coming games for both mixed, ladies or men's games, some held here at home and some away at a different bowling club and some of those games differed in as much as they were indoor or outdoor on the green.

'Right now, ladies,' oozed Pulse Dover through the tannoy system, 'on the red card, eyes down for a full house. And your first number is-'

'Old on! Old on!' squeaked Old Nick Chambers, running to the toilets, 'I aint ready! I lost me glasses in the loo!'

'I lost my glasses in the loo, once,' intoned Lily, 'me Lookers an you can't find Lookers with Readers an when I got em they was misty-'

'Oh, pooh!' cried the Blagett sisters.

'Exactly.' Lily responded.

'Here we go, then,' insisted Pulse at the number indicator, 'and the first number is: Four and Three; forty three.'

'Ooh, I've got forty three.'

'What did he say?'

'I remember forty three.'

'I aint got a pen.' Came the usual replies.

Eddy sat back and enjoyed the time. Club members having a good time in the homely atmosphere of their club house. He sat back with a smile. 'I hope you're not relaxing too much,' a strong voice boomed in his ear. Eddy jerked upright and found himself looking into the accusing stare of Aldous Hiller, who had sneaked his large bulk up on him with Price Watergate and Jason Cable. 'Keep yourself up and ready for Sunday's big game,' Aldous continued as he and his two committee men sat at the table, oozing into chairs, with Aldous's seat creaking under the great weight, 'we're relying on you to do the business on the Pilkington mob.'

'Yer, you gotta do 'em,' said the scruffy, unshaven Jason, scratching his chin, 'no matter what, we got to win.'

'Yes, old boy,' intoned Pricey, 'an emphatic win is required, to safeguard the honour of BUMs.'

'Yeah,' murmured Jason, 'kick their tired old butts.'

'Now, I have a cunning plan,' winked Aldous, 'we're taking a trip tomorrow, just us four. And we're going in Jason's pick up truck.'

'We are?' Eddy was confused, 'where to? And why?'

'Pilkington Bowling Club,' sneered the bloated President, 'we're going to see the strength of the opposition. Get yourself round here to the club at eleven tomorrow morning and we'll take a ride to Pilkington.'

'Is this something you do,' queried Eddy, eyebrows narrowed, 'before a game? Spy on the opposition?'

'You must realise, old boy,' Pricey explained, 'this final

game against Pilkingon is a very important match.'

'It's the big one.' Jason growled.

'You must understand,' Aldous wagged a finger at Eddy, 'there are two hundred and eighty bowling clubs in Cheswick county. Whomsoever loses the Sunday match between us and Pilkington, is the lowest rated club in our county. And it's *always* us! But this time, I'm going to change it, no matter what I have to do. Be here tomorrow.' The three left Eddy to finish his pint alone and bewildered.

While Eddy had been talking and planning with his co-conspirators the first half of the bingo had finished and now Horatio Anchor took to the microphone. 'And now,' his big booming voice matched his big, red face and shiny shaved head, 'it's time for the half time quiz. First question. First question; professional boxing, who is the world middleweight champion?'

'Marvellous Marvin Hagler!' shouted Kirkland Dunne with a laugh, from one of the tables.

'Correct!' cried Horatio.

'Marvin Hagler!' Eddy Edmunds retorted, 'but Hagler was world champion decades ago, three or four decades ago at that! Not now!'

'I know,' laughed Kirkland, as he called across the busy tables, 'Anchor gets his questions from the last copy of the Guinness Book of Records that he bought, years ago. I've got a copy of that issue as well. That's why I always win.' Eddy sadly shook his head in disbelief.

'Question two.' Horatio boomed out on the microphone, 'Question two; what is the fastest production car in the world?'

'Ferrari Enzo!' cried Kirkland with a grin.

'Correct!' Horatio called. Eddy couldn't believe what he was hearing. The questions rolled on and on with only Kirkland answering, and some of the club members were actually applauding Kirkland's superior knowledge!

At last the quiz was over and the Tweed figure of Lady's Captain Gladys Glendenning took to the mike. 'Ladies and Gentlemen,' she flashed a smile full of long teeth and popping eyes, 'it's time for the raffle. Hope you've all got your tickets? Here we go then.' She pressed a button on the number indicator. Eddy took a look at the two tables put together at the far end of the club house where the raffle prizes were sitting. A bottle of light white wine, bath salts, a pack of dusty Christmas crackers and a packet of jelly babies. He gave his raffle tickets to a poor-looking old couple sitting on their own and left the club for the night, he just couldn't stand the excitement of another raffle.

CHAPTER TWENTY

The next morning, Saturday, Eddy found himself standing in the small car park of the BUMs club, awaiting for the arrival of Jason Cable and his pick up truck. At first he hadn't understood why they had to use Jason's truck, then he realised; of course! Aldous would not even begin to get into a small family car, and if he did, he'd probably weigh it down on one side and the bodywork would scrape on the wheels.

An old scruffy American truck rumbled its way up the short lane from the road to the bowls club car park, its red body fringed with rust. It had four doors and an open space at the back in the truck style. The vehicle skidded to a halt in the empty car park by the side of Eddy, 'Jump in,' cried Jason, his long greasy tangled hair swinging as he leaned over, 'best get in the back, Adolf Hiller can't get in the back, the door's too narrow.' Eddy climbed in, grateful just this once for Aldous's bulk, as he could smell Jason's BO from the back seat, so it would be stronger in the front.

A door slammed in the BUMs club house and Aldous appeared, marched slowly up to the truck and opened the door and began a series of grunts and groans, along with puffing and blowing and lifting his legs with his hands, and then finally, with a heavy grunt, he was in. The truck took a long, soft droop down on the left side as the enormous President of BUMs relaxed into the seat.

Price Watergate walked into the car park from the lane looking like a gentleman thug with silver hair swept back, clean shaven and with sparkling brown eyes and pinky, scrubbed face. He wore a perfectly white shirt, thin black tie with a black suit with a dark red waistcoat and brightly shining boots. 'Good morning gentlemen,' he said with a royal wave as he jumped into the back seat of the truck beside Eddy. After much reversing and forward movement of the rusty old truck, Jason turned from the lane into the road and they were off.

The big V8 engine of the old truck growled as they dipped and floated on its long suspension under the weight of Aldous in the narrow roads of Upper Morten with its nineteen-thirties houses with pretty front gardens and fences. Then they were in Upper Morten High Street with its little boutique shops of fashion for the ladies, a pub-restaurant, charity shops, local supermarket, newsagents *et al*, all clean and freshly painted nose-in-the-air snooty style.

Then they were out in the open roads with green fields and meadows. 'Weather looks nice and bright today...' Eddy tried to find something to say in the moody silence of the truck's cabin.

'Listen,' barked Aldous, 'this aint no dainty day trip. We're spying. Spying on Pilkington Bowling Club to see what we can see. And we're looking for weakness, any weakness. Whatever we see may help us to win tomorrow. They must be stopped. This is serious. I am *not* going to be number two hundred and eighty again.

'Nah,' agreed Jason at the wheel, 'we gotta win at any cost.'

'Yes, this time,' commented Pricey, 'for the honour of BUMs, we must defeat the enemy.' The big truck swirled left at a large junction where a sign post informed them they were on route to the village of Pilkington.

At first on this road, the houses were scarce and far between, then they began to line the road more and more until, at the end of a lane between two large old houses, a small sign pointed to: Pilkington Bowls Club. They turned in to the lane. 'Quiet now, Jase.' Aldous commanded, and Jason took his foot from the accelerator pedal and let the big truck flow forward on idle.

Soon the club house could be seen over the hedge on the right hand side of the lane. It was an old club house, wooden framed with an asphalt covered roof and wooden veranda's. The truck engine burbled gently as they crept by. 'Get alongside the green and stop,' instructed Aldous in a whisper. The truck stopped close to the right hand hedge in the little lane behind the club and Jason switched off the engine. All was quiet.

'Just keep quiet for a while,' said Aldous, 'and make sure we haven't been seen, then we can make our move.'

'Move?' Eddy's eyebrows knitted together questioningly, 'move? What sort of move are we going to make?'

'Just wait for a while.' Aldous turned with a finger to his lips. Eddy gave up and decided to wait. The four sat in strange silence for twenty minutes.

'Right. Off we go.' Aldous ordered as he slowly and quietly turned the handle to open his door, and stepped, half slipped out of his seat. The truck gave a gentle, almost grateful heave as it raised itself up on its normal suspension setting as it settled itself back down. As the truck was on the right hand side of the lane, Jason couldn't open his drivers door, so slid across the front bench seat and followed Aldous into the lane. The two rear passengers did likewise.

Now all four were standing in the lane, Aldous and Jason pulled out the pins which locked the loading flap at the back of the truck, which they quietly and gently dropped to a level position on chains hanging from the back ends of the truck. Aldous turned and seated himself on the metal flap making the chains creak, then he rolled over and was now in the back of the truck. As he stood up, Jason followed, then Pricey. They turned to look at Eddy, who shrugged in bafflement and followed until all four were standing on the open truck back.

The BUMs men were now high enough on the back of the open truck to see over the hedge and inside the green of Pilkington Bowls Club. Their four heads slowly appeared over the hedge. 'Good grief!' Pricey cried, 'it's abandoned!' His three companions agreed with a quick inhale of breath followed by dropped jaws.

The old veranda was looking sad and creaky, the windows into the club house were dirty and misted, the white plastic tables and chairs on the veranda were old and muddy looking, while the asphalt roof covering looked ragged. The green was looking faded and brown in places, and the pushers and irons on the rinks were rusty. 'Look!' Jason hissed, 'here come a few of the good old boys.'

From the club house came seven people, four old men struggling to carry their woods, puffing and blowing through their moustaches and beards wearing grey trousers and whitish tops who were followed by three ladies, who were carrying cups and glasses, who sat at a nearby rickety table.

The men dropped their woods at a rink and after throwing up a jack, began to bowl, with their woods not getting up to the far end of the rink as they tiredly bowled. More people followed the first bowlers and watchers, some on walking sticks, and some needing help to get down to the green, all rolling their woods up lethargically. 'I think it's about time to go,' Eddy mumbled quietly to his co-spies, 'I just noticed some of the ladies pointing at us.'

'Yeah,' agreed Aldous, 'time to go.' He sat down on the truck back and rolled himself toward the end, where he sat in a sitting position with his legs dangling over the side, then stepped down. Soon all four were back sitting in the front half of the truck.

'Fantastic news chaps,' smiled Pricey, 'Pilkington look knackered. Should be good news for BUMs on Sunday if they turn up like that.'

'Yup,' agreed Aldous, 'could be good. I am *not* going to be number two hundred and eighty again. I was going to resort to terror tactics, but after what we've seen today, we stand a good chance of winning on highest points what with our superteam of Eddy's. Back to BUMs, let's get Dave to open the bar early.'

'So, here's me idea,' Kirkland Dunne stood at the bar later that day, wearing his red and white T-shirt and scruffy green track suit bottoms, large brandy in hand while he held court for all to hear, 'we phone Pilkington club house 'n' say we're a coach touring company, right? We say we've been hired by Teddy Adams, that's Pilkington's President, see? And we say we're picking up their team to take them to play at BUMs, to save the old codgers from driving all the way here.

'So, then we get the driver on the day to take them down the coast for a day out, and by the time they've been to the coast, explained to the driver that they're supposed to be here at BUMs it'll be too late. Game over. Of course, there'll be a few who will drive themselves here anyway, so they won't have a full team. And if they want to have a token game, well, I'll beat them on my own.'

'Yes, good plan Kirk,' sneered Aldous, sitting with Pricey at a nearby table, 'but no need, methinks. We had a look at Pilkington, and it's not what it used to be. Lots of old boys, and they're all well past it. Why, the place looks like its ready to fall down. I think this season, we're gonna make it to two hundred and seventy nine.' Aldous and Pricey gave royal waves to the tiny applause from the nearby tables.

Standing in the doorway to the kitchen, where he had been watching the Blagett sisters unfold and lay out the tables and chairs for the evenings yearly meeting of the Lady Players of BUMs, Jason Cable beckoned Jackson Irons over. 'What's up Jason?' asked the small, intense man, his large nose pointing up at Jason from his round face and white hair.

'Make a phone call, Jackson, you know, nice and discreet, like, to the local news paper,' answered Jason, 'remind them it's the last game of the season tomorrow, and BUMs against Pilkington is gonna be an exciting, really excellent final, sparking off a new era in bowling.'

'OK, I'll do it,' beamed Jackson, 'but I'll have to promise their reporter a drink or he won't turn up.'

'Cool, make it a large one.' Jason turned away.

Eddy had to squeeze into the little area by the main entrance to see the list of players for the big final game against Pilkington. Here on the wall was, at last, the list of members who would be taking up the challenge for BUMs. There was a real crowd of people in the small area pushing and shoving to see who had been picked to play, and Eddy tried as hard as he could to gently side step and manoeuvre his way through until he was at the front. He was pushed flat against the wall and could only see by peering up at the pinned-up notices. And there it was! He was number one with the three young men making up the superteam.

'Cool,' said Kirkland from the side of his mouth from amid the pressing crowd, 'someone's shown a bit of common sense. I'm skipping.'

'Ow come they aint got me with Horatio in my team?' demanded Old Nick Chambers, the little man's voice seeming to come from somewhere behind or below the crowd.

'Oh, pooh!' cried the Blagett sisters, 'we're on reserves.'

'That's cos someone's needed to move the tables round.' Amyzon Sirly laughed as she crushed someone against the wall.

'Is there a meal after the game?' asked Evelyn "2 cod" Brown, licking her lips. I hope it's fish and chips.'

'There won't be fish and chips on a Sunday,' scoffed Pulse Dover, rubbing himself up against a lady bowler, 'it'll be roast beef, I reckon.'

'Well I can't stay late,' said Lily Puddle to everybody, 'I'm going to Ginny's she's got the plumber round 'n' last time he was there his bum cleavage gave her palpitations so I'm sellotaping me lens on me Seers to check.'

90

'Shame,' said Evelyn, 'cos the chippy puts in extra chips, and I always get at them before anybody else.'

'Gather round the end of club, girls!' The Ladies' Captain, Gladys Glendenning cried out to the patrons in and around the bar, 'it's the annual gathering for the ladies' end of season meeting.' She ushered all the ladies round the tables laid out by the Blagett sisters and soon there were eight lady players seated, as most of the other ladies had disappeared as soon as the meeting was announced. Two of the tables had been pushed together and the women sat round the middle with GG Glendenning in the centre with pad and pen at the ready. Eddy Edmunds' wife attended for the first time.

'Well, let's first of all greet our new lady member,' sad GG, 'Mrs Juney Edmunds.' Juney looked up politely at all the other ladies at the table, her thick, dark hair curled around her olive-complexioned face, her dark eyes bright, her small turned-up nose above her smiling mouth. She wore a comfortable grey cardigan with black slacks and slip-on black shoes.

'Will there be any cake while we're here?' Evelyn asked, pushing back her thick glasses as she settled her barrel shaped bulk into her chair.

'No.' Winnie Wilson spat sharply, the yellowy skin of her arms flopping on the table top, 'we're here to talk about bowling.'

'Who's not here?' Amy Sirly asked, leaning forward and revealing the packet of twenty fags down in her cleavage.

'How about biscuits, then?' Evelyn asked the table in general. 'I could eat a biscuit or two.'

'Not much of a turn out is it?' Betty Blagett said.

'No, it's just the usual girls who always turn up,' answered Dotty Blagett, the sisters were both in their table moving outfit of white skirts and blue BUMs blazers, 'mind you there's one extra with Juney.'

'Well, I'm having trouble with me wooden leg,' started

Lily Puddle, 'it could be rot but when it comes off the table falls over.'

'Let's get down to business,' said GG in a low voice, 'what about that Enid Fulton? What behaviour!'

'That Enid Fulton!' Winnie exclaimed, 'she doesn't care what man's car she gets in to be taken home after a game.'

'An' when the table goes over,' continued Lily, 'the fish bowl goes as well I've got Freddie the goldfish in a tin mug.'

'Enid Fulton. Enid Fulton?' cried Betty, 'Enid Fulton? Whose she?'

'Enid Fulton, you know,' Dotty explained, 'Enid Fulton, she's been married *four* times.'

'Disgusting.' GG agreed, 'and she was hanging around the bar last night till closing time with all the men.'

'Hussy!' cried Winnie, 'she even smiled at Jason Cable when he bought her a gin and tonic.'

'Why have you got such a down on this Enid Fulton?' Juney asked.

'She's not here,' laughed Betty Blagett.

'And she is eighty seven,' giggled GG.

'Mind you,' murmured Lily, 'I did like her book The Famous Five.

'That was Enid Blyton,' GG said with a sigh, 'not Enid Fulton.'

CHAPTER TWENTY TWO

And so the great day dawned. Sunday. The big match! Eddy was as excited as he could be. It was to be his first final and he was going to be in a superteam! Eddy got to the club early, changed into his white shirt and trousers and got a refreshing pint from the bleary eyed Dave.

Eddy watched as the BUMs club house slowly woke up for the big match. First the Blagett sisters arrived and began to unfold the tables and put them in position for the after game meal. Then Amyzon Sirly arrived loaded down with carrier bags full of food and began to fuss around in the kitchen to the clattering of plates, knives and forks and warming ovens.

The club members poured in, pulling their wheeled bags and cases or puffing along carrying their woods and changes of clothes they would need for the game. The sun began to shine down on a very bright and warming day. In the car park Jackson Irons was directing traffic. 'Now come on!' Jackson shouted, directing all the BUMs club drivers, 'park across the available space using up all the room.'

'Why we got to do that,' asked a confused lady player, in her BUMs blazer and white skirt, 'there'll soon be no room.'

'That's what Aldous wants,' said Jackson with a finger tap on the side of his nose, 'that way the Pilkington codgers will have to park out in the road, beyond the yellow lines and have to walk all the way here carrying their woods and stuff.'

'I don't know why you bother with all that,' snorted the lady, as she shook her head and walked into the club house, 'it never worked before.' But soon the car park was full up, and down beyond the yellow lines, even the BUMs players had to park and walk back in.

Aldous and Pricey Watergate sat at one of the tables watching all the arrivals while in the changing rooms players got themselves ready for the game. In the busy men's room with lockers being opened and shirts and trousers being changed and bowling shoes being tied up or slipped on, old Charlie Higginbottom struggled to pull off his jacket and shirt, his thin and bony body showing the tufts of dirty grey hair springing from his ears and his nose in long grey whisps, but still sporting a shiny bald head. His thin lumpy frame, together with his floppy man boobs, pot belly and sticky-out bum and his arms and legs still had layers of flappy skin.

Charlie dropped his shirt and blazer onto a nearby bench and unbuckled his belt and dropped his trousers. 'Ooh,' cried Charlie with a grin, 'I've dropped me pants as well as me trousers. So now I'll have to bend right over and pick me pants up again.' Charlie stood naked in the crowded, bustling changing room, his saggy belly and droopy bum on show.

'No! No Charlie! Don't do it this time.' shouted the men in the changing room with a knowing laugh, 'we don't want to see! Don't bend down! Not again!' Too late. Charlie bent down with stiff legs to regain his dirty grey pants, sticking his horrible ancient bum up in the air.

'Eeuurgh!' shouted the men in the changing room, like a chorus, 'you do it every time Charlie!'

Kirkland Dunne changed out of his red T-shirt into a brighter T-shirt of flaming red and a pair of pink shorts and bright red and white trainers before going to the bar for a pre game large one.

In the middle of the busy changing room, Pulse Dover grinned at himself in the faded mirror, combing his grey hair and admiring his looks, 'Oh, there's bound to be some lovely old girls out there today, all for me!'

Horatio Anchor and Fergus O'Brien stepped through into the crowded changing room to boost morale, Horatio with a wave said, 'Good luck today, boys. Were gonna win this one, I can feel it in me water.'

'Gin this bum!' agreed Fergus with a grin.

In the ladies' changing room GG Glendenning squeezed her feet into her slip-on bowls shoes, stood, smoothed down her white skirt, brushed her hand over her short brown hair and said; 'I'm ready! Come on girls, let's go!' She grinned a toothy grin, 'today's our day.' No one took any notice.

The thin, frail looking whispy hair and yellowy skin of Winnie the witch Wilson rose slowly as she finished changing for the game, 'Well, I don't know what all the fuss is about. We always lose the final. Everyone knows.'

'Yes, I know,' said GG with a sigh, 'but we must try, musn't we?' Winnie shrugged her shoulders.

'Well, I don't know.' muttered Lily, 'this is like sleeping in the air raid shelter during the war well actually it was years after the war I was still sleeping in our air raid shelter 'cos Mum and Dad didn't tell me the war was over...'

Outside Aldous at last dragged Old Nick to the small alleyway between the changing rooms to where the large rubber-covered metal handle protruded from the wooden wall of the changing room. The handle was at the bottom where the label on the wall stated: ON.

'Now,' shouted Aldous, pushing Nick to the handle, 'when I say "Now", turn the handle.'

'Eh?' Nick asked, a hand to his ear, 'what'd you say then?'

'Oh, cor blimey.' Aldous stared into the sky, 'You stupid deaf old git! Listen: when I say "Now"-'

'Now?' asked Nick, getting angry, 'when you say "Now"?'

'Yes, you fool, when I say "Now"!' Crash! Nick slammed the handle into the up OFF position.

'No, no, you soppy old nutter,' shouted Aldous, 'I didn't mean now, not now, I meant do it when I say "Now", oh, Gawd help us, you've done it anyway.'

'It's too late to say now, now, isn't it?' Old Nick spat back in anger, 'you've already said now, now, and so now I've done it now already.'

The bundled up electrical fence was tossed into the alleyway between the changing rooms.

Eddy waited and, after a considerable time, was relieved to see the rest of his superteam arrive. Danny Mallet, Jermain Jones and Kenny Layton wandered into the changing rooms and stepped out looking like something a BUMs player should with white top and trousers and bowling shoes.

Amid the general bustle of the BUMs players who were ready to bowl, suddenly the cry went up 'Here comes the Pilkington team!' Through the gate from the car park walked a small crowd of elderly players, mostly men and a few ladies. They looked fresh and happy, no one was sweating or labouring under the heavy weight of woods or changes of clothes as they carried nothing. They all wore their blue blazer with Pilkington logo and a few badges.

To Aldous, they looked suspiciously happy. 'Ere, what's going on?' he demanded, 'why are you all so happy? And where's your gear, you're bowling clothes and woods that you'll need to play today?'

'Oh,' said Will Yates, a tiny little man who looked lost in his club blazer, 'we didn't have to walk from down the road or carry our stuff.'

'Why not!' Aldous demanded, smelling a rat, 'where's your cars? How'd you get here anyway?'

'Our young new team members dropped us outside,' explained Will with a wink, 'so we only had to walk through the car park, and when they've parked up they will bring our woods and stuff with them.'

'Your young new team!' exploded Aldous, 'what d'yer mean, young new team? When we had a look at you lot the other day there was only you old lot there, there was no one else!'

'Yes, well,' explained Will, 'we had a lot of old timers leave or retire from the game of bowls from Pilkington, so we spent most of the season training our new members, mostly the grand children of our old players, of course they can't play during the week because they have to go to work, so we trained them at the weekends only. And they've turned out to be great bowlers. They'll be here in a minute.' Will walked into the club bar with a muffled giggle. He was followed by half of the usual old folk from Pilkington, but there were a few faces missing. The missing faces would be replaced by the new young team Will talked of.

'Treachery! Aldous gasped, 'treachery on the last day of the season!' He quickly called his inner circle around and they sat in the bar window to watch the arrivals of the new team. Pricey, Fergus, Horatio, Jason Cable and GG Glendenning waited and watched.

BUM's News
The Offical Organ of Bowls: Upper Morten

Secretary's Plea

The annual match, where we fight against being the last Club in the League, is upon us once more. I beg all players to make themself available for this fixture, if not selected, please, please attend as a spectator to imtimidate Pilkington BC.

Over watering solved

After a month long investigation, the sub-committee of the garden working group, who reported to the main Committee via the gardening committee, reported.

Their report stated that they believe that it was rainfall was the only reason for the over watering, therefore it was God's fault. The Chair Person of the Garden Committee, stated that God had no right to interfere as he was not on the watering rota and he would not be added to it.

The above Committee has been asked to investigate the spate of flowers appearing in the flower beds which has become rife over the last few weeks. They will report in the autumn

---

A senior member of the Elite Bowling Squad has lodged an objection with the Board regarding the selection of players. He states, in his written submission, that he selected his playing partners in the interclub pairs, mixed pairs and triples and they had been ignored to a degree.

How could he win trophies when he had inferior players?

The Main Committee have called an special meeting to discuss his accusations. So an impartial judgement is not expected

Miscreant drummed out of Club

A Newbie was accused of bringing the Club into disrepute by a member of the Club's Elite. The accusation being, that he, the Newbie, had obtained a copy of the Club Rules and had read them! A charge that was strenuously denied. He claimed that the misdemeanour that he is arraigned for, is one of the unwritten rules that abound the club.

This fact he used as his main defence ' To gain access to the rules you either are classified as a privileged player and given them as rite or you learn by your mistake, which was the case here. ' he pleaded.

A Wallaby Court was held in the Great Hall, to consider the charge. After deliberating for some minutes the Court found the accused guilty as charged, this despite an impassioned plea for leniency from 'his friend in Court', who claimed that his associate was given to acts of misjudgement due to working in a trade that did not suffer fools gladly and where mental abuse was paramount

After the verdict was pronounced guilty party was frogmarched to the centre of the green, where his Club Badge was torn from his shirt and as tradition dictates, the sleeve of his bowling arm was half ripped off. The Chairman said after the court, that this judgement applied only to the bowling side of the Club and the culprit would be allowed to use the club at any social event & function or when the bar was open.

No appeal is expected

CHAPTER TWENTY THREE

Four young men stepped quickly into the car park carrying bags, bowls and pulling wheeled baskets of the older Pilkington bowlers. All four wore sunglasses and lightweight business suits and black shiny shoes, and all four averaged six feet tall with short dark hair. They chatted together in a quiet, confident, friendly manner as they walked, waving hello to all as they passed the window where Aldous and team-mates watched in wonder and horror.

'I think,' said Aldous with a shudder that shook the creaking chair that he sat on, 'we've been hit by the bowling Mafia.'

The four young men followed their older Pilkington players into the visitors' changing rooms. 'I want a Council of war.' Aldous said in a low, murderous voice, 'we must call a council of war right now. Let's get together round a table and see what we can do about being invaded by a superteam from Pilkington. Call my councillors here to this table now.'

'We are here already,' Pricey said in a shaky voice as he smoothed down his silver hair, 'we've all just seen what you've seen.'

'Treachery! Treachery, that's what it is,' said Aldous in a thunderous tone, 'they've pulled a fast one on us and called in a young superteam.'

'But that's what we were going to do,' Horatio spoke in a hushed whisper, his big red face glowing, 'we were going to pull a fast one and put our superteam in against the old codgers and they've done it to us.'

'Fitted carpets!' Fergus Mad Mick opined in a nasty way, 'prawns and fruit juice for afters an' all.'

'Tell Dave Sirly to close the bar,' instructed Aldous, 'or Danny Mallet will be too drunk to play bowls, especially against the team that Pilkington've sent here. And get the Blagett sisters to sort out the mess of electric fence in the alleyway between the changing rooms.'

Dave Sirly was drawing pints, serving wine and spirits as more and more people entered the club house, many just to see the grand final. The tables around the main area of the club and the glassed-in area were crowded, glasses of beer and lager tottered on table-tops and crisps and cheese biscuits sat in the spilt beer as the atmosphere built up for the big game. When Dave got the order to close the bar he was met with cries of panic and woe, but he was under orders, so he closed up.

Outside, Jackson Irons was laying out the scoreboards, jacks and irons and the teams were gathering round to see where the score books would tell them on what rink they would be playing, while the opposing teams met, smiled at each other, shook hands and exchanged polite insults.

On rink one, Eddy was not happy. His opposition team from Pilkington were not what he had expected. They were four young men, who looked totally at ease in their bright white tops and trousers with immaculate creases, and smart brown bowling shoes. All of the four wore dark sunglasses under their short haircut and smiled a deep friendly smile to everyone as they unloaded their woods, all of which were light blue and sparkling clean.

'Who's this lot?' Danny Mallet asked, draining his fifth pint and belching really loudly, and wiping his mouth with the back of his hand.

'Good afternoon,' one of the four stepped forward and shook hands with every one of the BUMs superteam, 'I'm Gerry, this is Truman, Giles and August. We only play at weekends because of our careers in the city of London financial district. But we've learnt to bowl and love it. Anyway it makes a change from making millions of quid for our employers. Ha-ha.'

After the usual introductory speeches from the two

captains, the game got underway, with Jermain unhooking his headphones and turning off his music as he looked unbelievingly at the opposition. The first two ends got off politely as each team warmed up. On Eddy's rink, one, at the beginning of the third end, Kenny Layton stared hard at Eddy and said: 'These four blokes are weird, they really worry me.' Eddy shook his head.

As the visiting superteam of Pilkington had scored one on the first two ends, they bowled first. Gerry aimed and let his wood go as if it sailed from his hand; it rolled quickly and smoothly down the rink, hit the jack square on and continued to roll with the jack in front of it to the end of the rink where the jack fell gently into the ditch and the wood stopped just above it still on the edge of the green.

Eddy tried to emulate that first shot but missed and his wood was scooped up from the ditch. Gerry's next shot stopped just in front of his first, making a blocker. Eddy's next shot was short. Each shot which followed, by Truman and Danny followed this lead with more woods surrounding the Pilkington woods at the end of the green guarding the jack.

When the Skips took their turn, Jermain bowled fiercely to smash through the surrounding bowls but it wasn't enough; Pilkington had four. Each further end compounded the situation, with Pilkington starting and getting a toucher and into the ditch with the jack and Eddy's team increasingly frustrated by the high efficiency of the opposition, the BUMs team resorted to trying to smash hard through the surrounded jack with most of their shots only knocking just a few of the woods out of the way and still lose the end.

Eddy took the opportunity to look at the scoreboards on the rest of the six rinks. On the next rink, number two, Kirkland Dunne was bawling at his team-mates for giving him no help. On rink three Lily Puddle talked non-stop to her team who were losing the will to live. The next rink, four, Jason Cable blasted his wood down with such power that it slammed into the ditch wall. On rink five, Gladys GG Glendenning jolly hockey sticked her way down the green, waving on her losing team. Eddy could see that all the BUMs rinks were losing terribly. 'Oh my Gawd!' he thought, 'all losing badly!' It was halfway through the twenty-one ends now and all BUMs teams were losing by a large amount, including his own, which was actually worse off.

'Oi! Oi!' a sharp voice called Eddy, 'what do you think you're up to? You're supposed to be flying along to a great win with your superteam.' Eddy turned to see a red-faced Aldous glaring at him from the side.

'Yes, *we* were to be the superteam,' wailed Eddy, 'no-one told us we were going to meet a real superteam.'

Aldous stamped back into the clubhouse. 'I'm not having it! Not again! I must be able to do something! I must stop Pilkington. We're losing worse than usual. I will not be number two hundred eighty again.' What could he do?

CHAPTER TWENTY FOUR

Walking back into the bar area, Aldous raved, 'We gotta stop the game!' he roared, 'I'm not having it!' The people crowded into the club house took no notice at all of Aldous, they were intent on watching the carnage outside, it was like Christians being fed to the lions, it was unmissable X-rated horror.

Turning back to the window and looking out onto the green, Aldous saw that the little macintoshed man, Old Nick had just finished hurling his two woods. Striding to the door and waving to the little man, Aldous beckoned him inside. 'Whassup?' cried the nasty one, 'what could you possibly want now? I've just bowled!'

'Have you seen the other score boards, other than the tragic story that is your own? Get Jason in here,' Aldous instructed the little man. Nick looked up at the enormous mountain that was the President of BUMs, then turned and ran for Jason Cable. Aldous sat on a stool at the closed down bar and waited for the little man to return and wondered how he could stop the disaster that was this final game of the season. He determined: death before defeat!

'Here we are boss,' puffed Jason as he approached Aldous, dragging Nasty Nick with him, 'what's wrong?' Old Nick leaned towards the two and cupped his hand behind his ear, so as to hear what on earth had caused Aldous so much distress.

'I've just had an urgent message from Delfton Bowling Club,' lied Aldous, 'and it's bad news; the wind is blowing towards us.'

'What?' Jason looked mystified, 'the wind's blowing towards us? What does that matter? Who cares?'

'I told you he was mad.' whispered Old Nick.

'The wind's blowing in this direction and it's bringing with it a tornado!' Aldous muttered urgently, 'we've got to stop the game. The tornado is ripping off roofs and turning over cars in the road, ripping up trees...'

'Well, I've never heard of anything like this in Cheswick,' spluttered Jason, 'what can we do?'

'Meteorological office says a tornado is on it's way,' explained Aldous, 'we've got to get the players off the green.'

'I thought you said Delfton Bowls club told you about the tornado?' Nick asked with narrowed eyebrows.

'Yes, yes,' said Aldous with a dismissive wave of his hand, 'we've got to get these people off the green before a tree comes down on them or something.'

'You'll never get them off the green now!' Jason raised his arm to show a large wet sweat patch under his arm. 'It would take a big shock of an announcement to get them off the rinks now.'

'A big shock of an announcement, eh?' Aldous stood up from the creaking bar stool, 'Dave! Dave!' he cried in a loud voice to the club Steward who was napping behind the bar with a half finished pint in front of him.

'Eh? Whassat?' Dave nearly fell off the tiny stool behind the bar, 'what's up now guv?'

'Open the bar!' Aldous instructed, 'now! And go out on the veranda and tell all our players in a loud voice that you're open!'

'Ooh, OK, OK,' Dave staggered to his feet and began to roll up the metal bar grill to open up, 'I'll do it.'

'Jason, get Jackson,' Aldous ordered, 'get out the electrified fence and begin fixing it in. That'll keep the buggers out. Nick, come with me, we'll turn on the electricity in the fence as soon as we can to stop them going back on the rinks.' Aldous stamped quickly out onto the veranda outside the club house dragging Old Nick with him.

Dave Sirly stood outside the club house door with a microphone in his hand, as he'd switched the mike over to the outside Tannoy system. Dave's voice crackled over the public announcement system: 'Ladies and Gentlemen. I have an important announcement to make: The bar is now open! And the first drink is on Mister President Aldous Hiller!' The players were shocked, bumping into one another and tripping over woods when they heard the shock announcement, and each and everyone of them raced for the club house bar.

The more cautious of the Pilkington players dived for safety or fell flat on their faces as the stampede for the bar began. The BUMs players dashed across the green to the now open bar for a once in a lifetime free drink from Adlous Hiller. The general scuffle to be first at the bar and first served before the order was rescinded was vicious, with much pulling, pushing and head butting, and that was only the ladies and the aged and infirm.

As he passed Dave Sirly on his way to the electric fence Aldous grabbed the microphone from the Stewards hand and stuffed it into his pocket. 'Come on Nick!' Aldous cried as he dragged and half carried the poor little old man, whose legs were pumping like skinny pistons as he tried to keep up with the bellowing President, 'we have to save BUMs from the ignominy of being the two hundred and eightieth team out of two hundred and eighty.'

He dragged the little man to the alley between the changing rooms and pushed him down to the big lever, which was pointing upwards towards the top in the OFF position. Nick grabbed the handle. Aldous drew back to the end of the alley where he could see the green. What he saw completely surprised him. All the BUMs players had left the rinks and the Pilkington visitors were trapped on the green as Jackson Irons and Jason Cable had already fixed in the fence.

Aldous pulled the microphone from his pocket, flicked the switch and his voice boomed from the loudspeakers. 'Ladies and gentlemen. Here is an urgent announcement: Farmer

Goldsmith has just contacted us to say his entire herd of pigs has just broken out of his farmyard and have escaped his land. They are heading this way on a rampage, all two hundred of them-'

'I thought you said it was a tornado?' cried Old Nick from the other end of the alleyway.

'Shut it!' boomed Aldous's voice from the loudspeakers, 'the pigs are smashing everything in their way, laying half of Cheswick countryside flat. We must evacuate the green, and right now, before the maurading hundreds of pigs get here.' Click! His voice was gone.

The Pilkington players, on hearing the terrible announcement suddenly panicked and were trying to get past the fence; some of the men were climbing over the fence, others were squeezing through the strands, while many of the ladies of a certain age were pulling the top strand downwards and, gripping their skirts tight around them were stepping over the fence.

'Nick! Nick!' Aldous cried as he turned towards the little man, 'No! Don't turn that handle!' Old Nick held the handle in both hands and was leaning away from the lever, all the better to throw his weight into swinging it down to the ON position.'NO! No!' cried Aldous, 'not now! Wait until I say NOW!'

'Eh? Whassat?' asked Old Nick, 'did you say NOW?'

'Yes-' Crash! Old Nick slammed the lever into the down position.

'O h my Gawd!' exploded Aldous, as the fizzing and spluttering and sparking of the electrical current slashed through the fence and the escaping Pilkington bowlers. Aldous squeezed his eyes together in horror as the screams of the players reached his ears, about the same time as the smell of burning flesh reached his nostrils.

Then his squeezed together eyes slowly opened and his

twisted mouth turned into a rare smile which in turn changed into a broad grin. 'Well,' he said through the grin, 'BUMs won't be two hundred and eightieth this year will they?

'Still,' his grin widened, 'that's bowls!'

THE END

What the papers said ▶

The County Clarion
Sports coverage wherever it happens

High Voltage game ends in a shock
by our Sports Editor Anthony Weyroc

Once again, BUM's contested the final position in the League, this year they entertained Pilkington BC, who's decline over the years was self evident. Up to the tenth end the 'Pilks' were having the far best of the match, however after that end, the dramatic finish began to unfold.

With the threat of marauding pigs devastating the countryside, which never materialised, the shout that the herd was imminent, coupled with the call that the bar was open, that stampede nearly finished the game, but it was the shout of 'Now' that switched on the electric fence, that's what did for Pilkington's.

The result has been placed in abeyance.

In an unprecedented move by the ruling Committee of the County Bowls Association have been forced to take advice from Bowls England after a formal objection was served upon them by Pilkington BC. It is believed that they have cited unsporting behaviour regarding parking facilities, the excessive use of free alcohol and the deliberate misuse of electricity which contravenes the Health & Safety Act.

Defending their rear, the BUM's replied, parking was due to too many spectators, the whiskey was offered in a spirit of friendship and people ignored the Warning Signs.

This column will report on any new developements this story.

Cricket	Football
Bedlington Village won the inter-county championship by beating their arch rivals, Toddington in a one sided affair. BVCC amassed a huge	County United have signed the ex-Chelsea, Aston Villa, Plymouth Argyll, Dundee United, Rotherham United and Watford central defender, Bill

WHAT THE PAPERS SAID

Electrifying Finish

Daily Telegraph

Freek Accident!

theguardian

Join our Crusade
- ban all electric fencing

MoS

Pilks shocked
by an AC arc

Wanganui Chronicle

NZ

SHOCKING RESULT

D<small>AILY</small> N<small>EWS</small>
BOWLING GREEN KENTUCKY

WERE ANIMALS HURT?

VETNEWS

<u>WHAT THE PAPERS SAID</u>

CURRENT TOO STRONG FOR PILKINGTON
Daily Express

Fail Safe - Fails
Gloucester
ECHO

HSO look into BUM's
Sun The

Electrical discharge kills off game
𝔖𝔶𝔡𝔫𝔢𝔶 𝔐𝔬𝔯𝔫𝔦𝔫𝔤 𝔥𝔢𝔯𝔞𝔩𝔡

Electric jolt from the Green
Report needed ?

Electrical Times

Stunned at BUM's
BORCHESTER ECHO

14172109R00066

Printed in Great Britain
by Amazon.co.uk, Ltd.,
Marston Gate.